I RUINED MY LIFE ... OR SO THEY SAID

It's Not What Others Think You Are

Dr ANNE BUTCHER

First published by Ultimate World Publishing 2020
Copyright © 2020 Dr. Anne Butcher

ISBN

Paperback - 978-1-922372-92-5
Ebook - 978-1-922372-93-2

Dr Anne Butcher has asserted her right under the Copyright, Designs and Patents Act 1988 to be identified as the author of this work. The information in this book is based on the author's experiences and opinions. The publisher specifically disclaims responsibility for any adverse consequences which may result from use of the information contained herein. Permission to use information has been sought by the author. Any breaches will be rectified in further editions of the book.

All rights reserved. No part of this publication may be reproduced, stored in or introduced into a retrieval system, or transmitted in any form, or by any means (electronic, mechanical, photocopying, recording or otherwise) without the prior written permission of the author. Any person who does any unauthorised act in relation to this publication may be liable to criminal prosecution and civil claims for damages. Enquiries should be made through the publisher.

Cover design: Ultimate World Publishing
Layout and typesetting: Ultimate World Publishing
Editor: Anita Saunders

Ultimate World Publishing
Diamond Creek,
Victoria Australia 3089
www.writeabook.com.au

TESTIMONIALS

Anne is a woman whose determination to reach her goals despite some perceived obstacles in life is inspiring! A compassionate and thoughtful colleague, Anne has overcome some life events from her teenage years which can result in crippling grief and shame, and has instead gone on to achieve her dreams as an accomplished and respected social worker with a PhD. Anne's resilience in overcoming challenges, from studying whilst living in a remote mining community, to go on to have a successful career helping others is a reminder that the sky is the limit. Anne's experiences and honesty provide refreshing examples of how with a little help, hard work and the power of determination you are able to build the life you want to have.

Dr Amanda Nickson, James Cook University

Told at 15 she had ruined her life, Anne Butcher reveals how the resilience she developed from living with disability in her childhood, together with her mother's unconditional love, gave her the determination to prove such woeful prophecies wrong. By the time I met Anne she was already well along the road to a great career in social work which she then enhanced by further overcoming her self-doubt and making her way as both a social researcher and a progressive manager in the Human Services. This book is a story of hope and courage. It should become a good example for those today starting out on the rocky road to turn their lives around from disadvantage and trauma.

Ros Thorpe, Emeritus Professor of Social Work, James Cook University.

So many people, particularly young people, are seeking examples to dispel the seeds of doubt that naysayers can instil when obstacles arise. Anne is a shining light in this respect as she candidly shares her experiences as a young person and her subsequent journey in a relatable way that engenders hope and inspiration.

Heather Lovatt
Associate Professor,
Queensland Centre for Domestic and
Family Violence Research
CQUniversity, Australia

DEDICATION

This book is dedicated to the loving memory of my mother, Barbara, without whom I would not be the person I am today.

DISCLAIMER

Some of the names of people represented in this memoir have been changed out of respect for their wishes and their privacy.

CONTENTS

Testimonials	iii
Dedication	v
Disclaimer	vii
Introduction	xi
Chapter 1: In the Beginning	1
Chapter 2: Seventies' Wild Child	15
Chapter 3: You Have Ruined Your Life	25
Chapter 4: Revolving Doors	35
Chapter 5: Toads and Princes	43
Chapter 6: Speck on a Map	57
Chapter 7: World of Possibilities	71
Chapter 8: Final Pieces of the Puzzle	87
Chapter 9: My Years as an Octopus	95
Chapter 10: The Unexpected Blessing	109
Chapter 11: My Blessed Life today	115
Chapter 12: What's Next?	123
About the Author	129
Acknowledgements	131
Speakers Bio	133
Offers and Call to Action	135

INTRODUCTION

This is a deeply personal account of aspects of my life. I have written this book for you, the reader, to understand that there will be many people in your life who want to tear you down, who ridicule you, who discourage you from taking certain directions in your life, who seem to want to cut you down, as it were. Particularly in Australia where the 'tall poppy syndrome' permeates our culture. The message of this book is—don't listen to any of them, believe in yourself. There are many others who will help you on your life's journey. You just need to know where to look for them, but they are there, waiting for you to ask.

I have often wondered what makes the difference between those children who are repeatedly called derogatory names and told very negative messages about themselves by significant people in their lives and go on to accept and believe those negative messages, and those who, even within sibling groups, may be imbued with those very same negative messages, yet they never accept them as their truth. In fact, they go on to do quite the opposite, by achieving to their fullest potential, in spite of those negative messages, proving them all to be wrong.

I believe it is that quality called 'resilience' and it has long intrigued me why some people seem innately to have it while others do not, even when they are from the same family. If you have resilience you will be more likely to bounce back from life's knocks but if you don't have resilience you are likely to accept negative self-perceptions and self-beliefs which, in turn, create a downward spiral of self-doubt, negative self-image, and lack of self-confidence and self-esteem. These are the very same negative self-messages and beliefs that come back to you throughout your life, usually at crucial times when you are trying to decide which path to take or which decision to make about important directions in your life.

Take heart though, there are many wonderful programs and support services available today to assist us all to find our inner resilience and enhance our emotional health and wellbeing.

My story is one where I found my inner resilience and used it to achieve goals which I would never have thought possible. I hope my story will help you find your inner resilience so you too can achieve your life's goals, and even goals you haven't yet imagined. This story is for you.

CHAPTER 1

IN THE BEGINNING

When I think of Brisbane what comes to mind is beautiful sunshine, the snaking, muddy Brisbane River weaving its way around the city, and the beautiful Jacarandas in springtime displaying their glorious carpets of wondrous lavender blooms across the lawns and streets for all to see and admire. My earliest recollections of life are in this city where I was born and of the highset white and pink Queenslander home in Toowong, where I lived with my family. Life was good.

I was blissfully oblivious to the complexities of the world surrounding me, as every four-year-old should be. I was engrossed in what I was doing: playing with the boys, my older brother, Robert, and our cousin, James, as we drove our Matchbox cars along the many dirt road tracks and obstacle courses we had made in the soft bull dust under our house. It was 1962. I am the eldest daughter of our sibling group of four, having also a younger sister, Julie, and younger brother, Nick. The girls, bookended by the boys in our family.

This was the time when Robert Menzies was the prime minister of Australia, the Beatles had their first hit song, 'Love me Do', and the beginnings of not only a music revolution but a youth cultural revolution was being rooted within the fabric of Australian society. Some older folk, of my parents' generation, would say the ways of this generation of youth were outrageous, with their loud music, boys with long hair down to their shoulders or longer, non-conformist dress, drug taking and simply just 'way out' behaviours. Only upon reflection, in later years as an adult, have I come to realise what a significant influence this culture would have on me, in my teenage years to come.

We were not wealthy, just an honest, respectable, working class family. I lived with my mother, Barbara, and father, Terry; our paternal grandfather also lived with us, who we only ever knew as Bob. We never called him Granddad or Pop or Poppy. It was always just Bob, but we thought nothing of this as it was just the way it was. It wasn't until I was much older that I pondered how unusual this was, in comparison to other families, but nevertheless, in our family, it was accepted as totally normal. Bob was a big part of my life as a young child, I think perhaps because he often babysat for my mother when she was away doing errands, either shopping or taking one or the other children to doctor's appointments, or when she was in hospital having my younger siblings.

I remember in 1962 my mother returning from hospital with our youngest sibling, who was all wrapped up in a soft, blue, satin-edged bunny rug, wearing a white crocheted bonnet. I was standing on my tippy toes peeping over my mother's lowered arms to see a small, red, round face with eyes shut—what looked to me to be a little doll—cradled in her hands. My mother announced, "This is your little brother, Nick." There is an age difference of exactly two years between all four siblings in our family, so he is four years younger than me.

In the Beginning

My father worked for the Postmaster-General's Department, or the PMG, as it was commonly referred to back then. He was a hard worker and had studied at night school to work his way up the ladder in his career. He started out as a postman in Mount Isa where he met my mother. They married and had my older brother in Mount Isa before the family moved to Brisbane so he could take up a higher-level, better-paying position in the PMG. That's when he decided to do further study to position himself for further career advancement, which is exactly where his career trajectory took him, and us along with him. I always respected my father for studying to better himself and although his relationship and mine, as I became older, became very strained, I know I am a lot like him.

He was always at work when I was little but when he was at home in the evenings and on weekends my very earliest memories of him were as a loving and affectionate father. We children would sit on his lap in the evenings after tea (as we called it) while we all watched TV. He would carry us to bed when we fell asleep on his lap, or on the lounge, or the floor, and he'd be giving us kisses on our foreheads all the way to bed. This was my memory of him as a small child; it would have been nice if it could have stayed that way for all of my life.

Mum was a very practical, no-nonsense, straight-talking, hardworking woman for all of her life. She always sewed our clothes, knitted our winter jumpers, cooked all of the family meals and kept the house immaculately clean. She was not an overtly affectionate mother but we all knew she loved us unconditionally and would always do anything for any of her children.

"She's a tomboy," my mother would say. Off playing with the boys, climbing in the trees behind our house on a spare block of bushland that butted up to our backyard fence. I loved nothing more than swinging off a rope tied to a tree branch, or playing with little Matchbox cars in the dirt, or going to the shop at the end of our street to buy a cordial ice block, or a packet of mixed lollies, with the threepence Bob had given me. This was one of many very endearing memories I have of Bob. I would just take off on my own, with no fear in those days, to buy my lollies or ice block and walk back home eating them on the way. Sadly, it wouldn't be safe for small children to do this on their own in today's world.

I loved feeding the 'pet' magpie that flew in whenever he was hungry and needed a feed. We called him the very original name of Maggie. We only assumed he was a 'he'. We had no idea really, but along with our chooks, cats and our dog, Cuddles, these were my early childhood pets, which I remember with much affection.

Life was blissful in these early years of my life. Although, as a four-year-old, I do vividly recall a near-drowning experience in a little creek in Toowong which my brother, Robert, and cousin, James, and I were going to cross, which was usually a small trickle of water in a little gully, but on this particular occasion it had rained heavily just a little earlier that day. When we got to the creek it was a fast-flowing torrent. We stood there for quite a while wondering if we could cross when a boy in a scout's uniform approached the creek from the other side. He stood and surveyed the fast-flowing water then he began to make his way across the creek. Once he reached our side, I thought to myself, that looked pretty easy, so I decided to step out into the water to begin to cross the creek myself. Within a second, I was being quickly washed down the muddy creek. I was desperately grabbing on to the long clumps of grass at the side of the gully while struggling to keep my head above the rushing water. I couldn't swim and the gully flowed under a road bridge just a little further down the way, so it was a very dangerous situation. Suddenly, seemingly from nowhere, a hand reached down and grabbed my arm, pulling me out of the water. It was the boy scout who saved me. I was only a small child but I remember the feeling of utter relief

In the Beginning

I experienced at that time. I will never forget that near-drowning experience and the fear I felt that day. It has made me fearful of drowning ever since but I did go on to learn how to swim, so I am not fearful of water or swimming, just the thought of drowning.

In 1963, I began Grade One at the local Catholic primary school in Toowong, St Ignatius, and settled into school life quite well there. My big brother, Robert, also went to the same school, so I was familiar with going to and from there with Mum when we walked Robert to school before I started there. My mother never got her driver's licence or drove a car and at that time we didn't even own a car. It wasn't until years later that Dad bought a car.

I remember one occasion, during my first year at school, I was running late for school and in those days, there were all types of household street vendors operating from the back of their trucks. Vendors such as those delivering milk or selling bread, or fruit and vegetables regularly hawked their wares in our street. On this particular morning, it happened to be the baker who had turned up to deliver bread to our house. As I was late for school, my mother asked him if he would drive me there. The baker didn't hesitate; he helped me into his truck and took me to school, dropped me off, then I assume he resumed his house delivery rounds. Quite amazing that he didn't think twice to help my mum out in driving me to school, and even more amazing that she'd asked him to do it at all, because they weren't necessarily good friends, or even knew each other very well! As an adult, I reflect on this as a vivid and somewhat amusing recollection of that event.

It was during my first year at school that I was in a school play, *The Wizard of Oz*, and I was cast as the Wicked Witch of the West. I had long, wavy, white-blonde hair and wore a black satin dress and black jiffy slippers with sparkles on them. I was even allowed to wear some makeup and lipstick. I felt quite elegant and very special, all dressed in my beautiful satin dress, which I swirled around in when I first put it on. I had to remember though that I was a mean, nasty witch in the play, which was held in the school hall. As I walked around the stage while playing this role, the teachers, who were all Catholic nuns, noticed I was limping a little. After the play one nun commented to my mother about this and asked why I was limping. My parents later told me they had also noticed that there were times when my father was carrying me to bed in the evenings, after falling asleep in front of the TV, I would sometimes cry out in my sleep. So, with the nuns now also noticing my limp, my parents decided it was time to take me to the doctors to get this looked into further to see what the problem was.

After a visit to the GP and having X-rays taken, my mother was given a referral for me to be seen by a paediatric orthopaedic specialist, Dr Gallagher, and I remember the big adventure of going into Brisbane city, on the trams, past the beautiful, big, gothic-looking brick museum and on to the Royal Brisbane Children's Hospital. My mother and I were sitting in the waiting room for our turn to see the specialist when out walked a young boy who was on crutches, with his mother. His leg was strapped into a leather brace around his calf. This had another long leather strap attached to it which at the other end connected to another large leather chest brace, held on at the front with a lot of small metal buckles. It looked very strange as I'd never seen anything like it before and from my mother's comments, neither had she. She jokingly said, without thinking for one second that this could also possibly be my fate, "I hope you don't have the same thing that poor little boy has got" and I remember thinking, "I hope not too." Not for a minute did either of us think that could possibly be what might be in store for me. We were both wrong.

We were called into the doctor's room next. We got up, walked in and sat down on chairs in front of the doctor's desk. He was reviewing papers and held up the X-rays I'd previously had taken, while he examined them. Then he asked me to get up onto the doctor's examination table and he manipulated and moved both of my legs and hip joints up, down and sideways. Then he said I could return to the seat beside my mother. He looked at my mother and asked her, "Did you see that little boy who came out of my surgery before you came in?" and my mother said "Yes." He then said, "Well, she has the same condition that he has."

My mother sat looking shocked and speechless, staring at him. I looked at her for reassurance because I wasn't sure what this all meant for me, but I could tell from her reaction that it wasn't good. He went on to say, "She has a bone condition called Perthes Disease and it affects the hip joint of growing children. The blood flow does not sufficiently reach a particular hip joint for some unknown reason, and the bone which is the head of the femur does not form properly due to lack of blood supply. It is therefore soft and can easily be pushed out of shape if the pressure of walking upon it is not removed while the bone is still growing and developing, so that is what must happen."

He continued: "She must not put pressure on her right hip joint until the bone hardens, at which point it will harden sufficiently that she will no longer need to be kept from putting pressure on it. This should occur at around age 12." I was five years of age at the time.

He handed Mum some paperwork and we left the doctor's room. I wasn't sure what was going on while my mother appeared to be still in shock, yet she was going through the motions of following the instructions of what the doctor had told her we needed to do next. We went straight to the section within the hospital where they make prosthetics and all manner of aids for patients. I was measured up for the leather harness we had seen the little boy wearing and I was also given wooden crutches to use from that day onwards. It was all very strange for me because unless I twisted my leg, affecting my hip, a certain way, I was not in any pain. It just seemed bewildering why I now had to use crutches when my leg didn't feel any different to me. My mother explained it all to me so I could understand but as a child a lot of it washed over my head and it wasn't until I was much older that I fully realised what this meant for me. I just knew I had to do what I was told to do and that was to not walk using my right leg. It had to be kept off the ground. I had to use the crutches and my left leg only.

After receiving the crutches, it was not long before I had to go back to the hospital to try on the new leather harness, especially made for me. It fitted and I left the hospital wearing the harness, right leg strapped up to the back of the harness which buckled up around the front of my chest. It was held in position by two leather straps, one over each shoulder, stopping it all from slipping down my little body. I went home with Mum and from that day, for the next four years, I was to wear the harness and use the crutches every day, but being the previously active child that I was, I soon found out that there were ways around these new restrictions I was confined to. For the next four years my mother's catch cry was, "Anne, get off that leg."

I started Grade Two in Maryborough, Queensland, as my father had been promoted in his work and our family moved there in time for me to commence the new year. I attended St Mary's Catholic Primary School where I finished the remainder of my primary schooling up to Grade Seven. My recollections of being at that school were that the nuns were quite cruel and I was sometimes slapped with a ruler on my unstrapped leg if I got my spelling wrong. I do recall one time in Grade Six when I was punched in the back by the nun who was looking over my shoulder as I was completing a maths problem, and clearly I was not doing it correctly, but the first I knew of it was when I felt the closed-fisted punch hit the middle of my back. I was never good at maths. I have often wondered why the nuns were so cruel to small children, but it is perhaps a reflection of how they were brought up in Ireland, as many of them were young Irish nuns.

The children at school were very curious about why I was wearing all of the leather gear and using crutches and they would often ask if they could "have a go on the crutches", which I was happy to oblige. The problem was, they didn't always bring them back, so I would unbuckle all of my leather harness and then walk to find where the crutches were. Or, the other thing I would do was walk on my knees, which of course defeated the purpose of trying to keep the pressure off my right hip. Both of these workarounds to my mobility problem were big 'no nos' but what else could I do without having the crutches to rely on?

The children at school did call me names like 'peg leg' or 'spastic' or other horrible names as children do, but I didn't really let that bother me at all. I would talk to Mum about it and she would just say, don't listen to those children, they don't understand what they're talking about. So that was good enough for me and as a result I didn't think of myself as being disabled at all and I don't think anyone in my family thought of me as that either. So, I didn't feel that I was labelled in any way and consequently, I didn't develop any negative self-perceptions, which I now realise is unusual but still a very good thing indeed. In fact, it did not occur to me until many years later, when I became manager of the State Government Department of Disability Services in Mackay, that I'd had a disability as a child, which, as it has turned out, has had life-long physical implications for me.

On a more positive note, at primary school I do remember Easter time with great fondness. When there were chocolate Easter egg hunts held on the school grounds, and I couldn't run to find the eggs like all the other children, after all the kids had taken off to find the eggs the teachers would whisper in my ear exactly where to find the eggs. So, I would slowly saunter off on my crutches and head towards the trees or seats or the other places I had been directed to find the eggs. I thought that was pretty good and I think I was a little smug about it too as I sat and ate those chocolate eggs while the other kids were still running around and looking in all the nooks and crannies of the very large school grounds.

From Grade Two to Grade Four I had regular check-ups with doctors and specialists and, as I grew, new harnesses had to be made to fit me. The length of my wooden crutches had to also be extended to equally match my growth spurts. However, after four years of using this method of trying to make me keep my body weight off my right hip joint and not put any pressure on it, the improvisations I had regularly manoeuvred to counteract my mobility restrictions had, sure enough, adversely affected the hip joint. The regular X-rays were showing the damage being done to the head of the femur. It was becoming misshapen and was looking more oval-shaped than perfectly rounded, so more drastic and restrictive measures were needed. I was sent to be measured for a 'Forrest Gump' type of metal brace which I could not so easily take off. Once I was in it, there was no way I could use my right leg at all. It was fixed in place and it was quite a contraption.

I had to put my foot and right leg completely into, and through, a metal circular-shaped piece, which was covered in soft leather. When the calliper was fully in place, the leg side bars extended all the way to the top of my right leg where they attached to the circular metal piece near my hip. The soft leather at the top of this brace was there to make it more comfortable for me and reduce the pain from my body rubbing on it when I walked. At first it hurt a lot, but after a while I got used to it, so it didn't hurt so much as time went on.

Two metal bars extended from the top down both sides of my right leg, which had a leather knee patch to stop me from bending my leg so it was kept straight at all times, and my foot just dangled in the air above a metal foot plate which was what I walked on. The other foot then had to also be raised, to level me out, so I had to wear a specially made elevated orthotic leather boot on my left foot. The boot had descending from it two metal pieces about the same thickness as the bars on the side of my leg (one extended from under my toe area and the other under the heel); these were attached to a separate flat metal foot plate which is what I walked on.

"My siblings and me ready for school"

I wore all of this paraphernalia for the next three years except for when I took a bath or slept at night. It did its job though, and I was much more restricted in using my leg in any way at all. My mobility slowed down a lot. I couldn't scoot off on my crutches as I had been able to do before. I could only walk fairly slowly now or I would have toppled over. Neither could I work out any improvisations to work around this contraption. It had me locked in good.

In school, I sat at a small table which was set at the front of the classroom, where there was more space for me to swing my right leg to put it up or down onto a small wooden stool which was positioned in front of the table for this purpose. I didn't really mind being there but it did mean I was always set apart from the other students, and also right under the teacher's nose.

I think I was a fairly good, obedient student, but academically I was just average and mostly got average grades. I never really got up to any mischief in primary school. I don't think I was able to, even if I wanted to. I was very restricted both physically and within the strict confines of Catholicism which I was subjected to at school and at home. Almost every school report card I'd ever had said I was capable of doing better if I put my mind to it. I was a bit of a chatterbox in the classroom so did get distracted easily.

In Grade Seven at the age of 12 and after many X-rays and doctor's visits throughout my primary school years, my parents were told by the doctors that the bone in my right hip had hardened as much as it was going to, and I could now do away with all of the callipers and be allowed to run free and have a normal life. I was so excited. I know I wanted to do everything, all at once.

My parents gave my sister and I pushbikes for Christmas that year, so I rode my bike everywhere. I took myself off and joined a trampolining club and a netball team and a basketball team and while I wasn't any good at any of these sports, because I still had a limp, I enjoyed the freedom of being able to run and do things I hadn't been able to do before, without my mother yelling at me,

In the Beginning

"Anne, get off that leg." Poor Mum, if she had a dollar for every time she said that to me, she'd have been a wealthy woman.

I do look back on the year I was able to be free at last and how I rode my bike all over Maryborough and registered myself for all the sports that I did. I thought nothing of it at the time but looking back now, I can see I must have always had a strong sense of self-confidence, to just go and do all of these things by myself without any adult being with me. I was not discouraged from doing these things by anyone either. If I said I needed a certain amount of money to register for a particular sport, I was always given it and I would ride back and pay the money to sign up. I also rode my bike to visit my best friends from Grade Seven. One, Dianne, lived nearby to my home but the other, Ludwina, lived on the far side of town. I didn't mind, I rode that bike everywhere with such a strong, satisfying sense of freedom.

I have often wondered where life has taken those primary school best friends or if they are even alive now. We lost contact when my father was again promoted in his career and was transferred from Maryborough to Mackay at the end of 1970. This was to become the next significant period of my life but for very unexpected reasons.

CHAPTER 2

SEVENTIES' WILD CHILD

We arrived in Mackay in December of 1970. It was the beginning of summer and it was very hot. We drove from Maryborough in our white and brown FB Holden station wagon which Dad had eventually bought while we lived in Maryborough. It was packed to the hilt, and along with Mum, Dad and us four kids, there was also the cat and our dog, Cuddles.

It was a very cramped, long, sticky, hot trip as these were the days before cars had air conditioning and it was summer in the tropics, so not only was it hot but it was also very humid. The whole trip was an uncomfortable experience for us all. We had many stops along the way to break it up but I know my father wanted to arrive in Mackay in the early evening as he wanted to show us the bright street lights and palm-tree-lined Nebo Road as we drove into the town for the first time. He wanted to give us a good, lasting first impression of how pretty this town was, which he succeeded in doing, even though we were all tired and wanted to get out of the car.

Dad had been promoted to the manager's position of Telecom (now Telstra) in Mackay. Previously, there had been no Telecom business site in Mackay, so he was there from the very beginning and he oversaw the development of every aspect of Telecom in Mackay from its inception through its many incarnations and changes to eventually become Telstra. He remained as the manager of Telstra until he retired in 1986 at the age of 60.

Life started out quietly in this new town and we kids were all enrolled in our respective new Catholic schools. My younger siblings were enrolled in the nearest Catholic primary school and my older brother in the Christian Brothers College. I was enrolled into Grade Eight at Our Lady of Mercy College, an all-girls school, for the commencement of the school year in 1971. I soon made many new friends there, some of whom I am still great friends with to this very day. We still keep in close contact which is very special, I think, as that isn't always the case for many people.

Again, the Catholic nuns were very strict at this school and between them and the strictness of Catholicism practised by my father at home, it meant my life was very closely reined in but it wasn't until I reached high school and adolescence that I started to feel this more than ever. I began to resent this strictness more and more and I was also beginning to question my religion for the first time in my life.

My first year at high school saw me as the usual compliant child that I had pretty much always been to that point but as I moved into Grade Nine the rebellious side of me was beginning to appear. I noticed at church every Sunday that the seemingly most pious people there were, as I would overhear the gossips say, the ones having the affairs, or the ones being charged with fraud for stealing from their employers, or those who would beat their wives. They would turn up to church as though they were the pillars of the church community. Then at home my father was drinking more and more. He had always been a big drinker on the weekends but as a smaller child I was more oblivious to his fits of anger and outbursts towards my mother which had happened from time to time in Maryborough too but had escalated, at least from my level of awareness, after we moved to Mackay. I remember one Saturday night after he'd had his day of following the races, gambling and drinking that he came home from the pub and asked what Mum had cooked for dinner as there was a big pot of food on the stove top. She said it was curried prawns which we all loved but he didn't like seafood, so he flicked his cigarette into the pot and said he wasn't going to eat that shit. Mum scooped all of the cigarette and ash out of the pot and we still ate it. Mum made Dad something else to eat.

Mum, Dad and Bob all punted on the racehorses. Saturday afternoons meant a constant drone of racehorse talk and race calling on the radio and I hated it. I never listened to what they were saying. I had no interest in the races at all—still don't. So, the radio was just constant, annoying background noise to me. Every time I attempted to talk or ask a question, I was told to shush up because the races were on. To this day I hate the races. My father would say, "We can listen to you anytime but this bloke isn't going to say it again."

There were many occasions of Dad coming home drunk on the weekends and being very verbally and physically abusive towards us all. There were many times when my brother or one of us would try to intervene to protect Mum but that only ended in a huge domestic incident. It is a wonder the police were never called to our place by the neighbours, but they weren't. As a teenager, I knew that home was not the place I wanted to be on the weekends, so I would often go over to my friends' places, just to get out of the house.

During the week Dad did not drink and he held down a responsible position and was seen by those who did not know what went on at home as such a lovely man. Which, of course, he could be at times, but when Bob moved to Mackay to live with us again (he'd stayed in Brisbane when we moved from there to Maryborough) and the two of them got on the drink together at the pub every Saturday and then again for both of the Sunday sessions, it didn't usually end very well. They would argue with each other. Dad would be verbally abusive towards Mum and all of us kids and we couldn't ever speak back as Dad was always right, although if I ever did speak back, I usually got into more trouble with Dad.

Grade Nine for me in 1972 was a time of observing the amazing cultural revolution that was going on around me in society and as I saw reflected in the media. As a 14-year-old, I was on the cusp of it all. I wasn't directly part of it. I was too young, but I knew what was going on around me and it was a very exciting time to be alive, for me and my school friends. It was the time of sexual liberation for women, with the pill being made available in the late 1960s for women to have some control, for the first time, over their own reproductive decision making. It was a time of the hippies and Hare Krishnas chanting on street corners. A time of conscription to the Vietnam War for young men, of the street protest marches against the war. There were slogans everywhere of 'Make Love, Not War' and 'Peace' with peace signs painted or worn in jewellery; there were Flower Power slogans. There was tie-dyed clothing, smoking dope, long hair, hippie fashions and the music of John Lennon, Creedence, Russell Morris, Daddy Cool, The Eagles, Neil Young, Skyhooks and so many more. *Countdown* was compulsory viewing on Sunday evenings. It was a heady time to be alive as a young and impressionable teenager, who was looking on from the sidelines but wanting to be in the thick of it all.

Of course, my father thought all of this youth culture nonsense was just rubbish and all these young people who were behaving in this way were just ratbags, and all this new music was nothing more than screeching and not real music at all. He and I were poles apart, which is probably not that uncommon for teenagers and their parents. I was much closer to my mother, as she seemed to understand me more and was more tolerant of my views on many things.

I remember wanting to do all the things that other young women were doing, at least what my friends were doing. I wanted to shave my legs and pluck my eyebrows and use tampons, but my father said no to all of these things. I wanted to go to the annual show with a group of my friends, which included boys coming along too, but my father said no to that. It seemed that no matter what I wanted to do my father said no. I realised in later years he was only trying to stop me from growing up but that was never going to be possible. In the end, I thought, why is it that a man can decide when I can do things that are really decisions to be made within the realm of women? My mother wasn't objecting to me doing these things, only my father. I decided he, as a male, didn't have any right to tell me, a female, not to do these things, so I just started to do them anyway. I shaved my legs, plucked my eyebrows and used tampons, if I wanted to. He didn't even notice or know any of it at all. I wondered what the big deal over all these things was for in the end?

It was during Grade Nine that I also started to notice boys. When my older brother came home from his all-boys school in the afternoons many of his school mates would come with him. We often had lots of young people at our house after school or sometimes on weekends, if Dad wasn't home. It was all just good fun and, while there was a little eyeing each other off and flirting, there was never anything in it at all at that time.

My mother was an amazingly strong woman who worked as the cook at the local fast food takeaway and convenience store for 20 years. After that she worked as the cook at the local hotel nearest to our home for another couple of years. In both of her jobs she always worked split shifts every day and in between shifts, she'd come home and cook dinner for the family, then she'd clean the house, do the laundry and the gardening, or whatever else needed doing. She never sat down to have a break or take it easy in those days. In the evenings when she came home from her second shift for the day, around 8.30 p.m., she would start doing the ironing and would iron until midnight. We sometimes had boarders, my brother's mates, living with us at different times and she cooked and cleaned for them too. She never complained about all the work she was doing or asked us to help her. She just got on with it herself.

I don't know how she did it all. She always cooked a hot breakfast for our family every morning before school and work. Dad always drove to work and we all rode our bikes to school. As Mum had never driven or held a driver's licence, if she ever needed to go anywhere when Dad wasn't at home, and before we kids could drive, she would get a lift with a neighbour with whom she'd become very good friends. This neighbour was very good to Mum, especially on occasions when Dad was drunk and abusive on weekends. Mum would sometimes go there to get away from him. She knew he would not go to the friend's house and cause a scene there. His abuse towards Mum or any of us when he'd been drinking was always behind closed doors at our house, so others couldn't see. As I got older, I didn't like to invite my friends over on weekends because I never knew how Dad would be or what state he would be in. I couldn't risk being embarrassed in front of my friends.

I did have a boyfriend in Grade Nine, my first boyfriend, which was purely platonic and nothing more than hand holding. That relationship finished almost as quickly as it started but it got me interested in the male species. All my girlfriends were starting to pair off with boys and as 14-year-olds, most girls in my circle of friends had boyfriends who were a few years older than them, around 17 and 18 years of age. It wasn't unusual then for male partners to be three or four years older than the female. As adults this is not such a big difference but in the teenage years it is a much bigger deal, as I was to find out.

Towards the end of Grade Nine or beginning of Grade Ten I met and fell for an older boy. He was not one of my brother's mates but he was very flattering towards me which was a new experience for me. Of course, I still wasn't allowed to be anywhere near boys and my father knew none of this at all as he would never have allowed it. I don't think my mother knew initially but she came to realise that I had a boyfriend.

Every Saturday my sister and I were allowed to go to the movies with our girlfriends, who were also sisters. We really enjoyed getting dressed up to go out on our own together. One of our fathers would drop us off and the other father would pick us up at the end of the night.

We often went and watched the movies together and had a good time but, over time, as a couple of us had started to have boyfriends, we planned that we would all go our separate ways after being dropped at the movies and meet up with our respective boyfriends. We all knew what time we had to be back at the movies before our fathers were due to pick us up but one night I got back too late and my father was already there, parked in the middle of the street with all the other girls in the car, and the cinema was in darkness. I got dropped off by my boyfriend who then took off in his car. I knew I was in very big trouble. I felt sick in the stomach. My father got out of the car and came up to me and asked me where I'd been. Without even answering he slapped me across the face and I fell to the ground in the middle of the street. I knew I shouldn't have gone off with my boyfriend and I'd been caught out. I got in the car and we went home. I wasn't allowed out again for a very long time.

On another occasion I snuck out to the midnight-to-dawn drive-in theatre with some of the local neighbourhood friends who owned cars. I had stacked my bed with clothes to make it look like I was in bed asleep. Everyone in the house was asleep and I was looking out the window waiting for my lift to arrive when my sister woke up and asked me what I was doing. I knew she would tell on me, so I said, "Do you want to come to the drive-in with me and our friends?" and she said, "Yes", so she packed her bed with clothes too and we both snuck out to the drive-in theatre.

We had a fun night with our friends but when they drove us home at dawn, as we got nearer to our house I could see all of the house lights were on and Dad's car was reversed into the carport, which it never was. It was ready for him to drive out quickly, if needed. When the car we were in pulled in near our house to drop us off, Dad's car lights came on and I yelled out, "Don't stop, keep going." So, they pulled out quickly again with Dad in hot pursuit. I thought he would kill us and them all. They drove very quickly around the block with Dad trailing behind us. When we got to the front of our house again, I said, "Pull over and let us out," which they did before taking off at speed down the street. My sister and I raced up the front stairs and into the house where our poor mother was there waiting for us. Of course, she asked where we'd been and what we'd been doing and we told her. She said, "Your father is going to kill you," which we already knew. Then we had the agonising wait for him to come home and we knew we would both get a belting for it, which we did. As the oldest I copped it first and the leather belt stung my legs many times. The belt buckle also cut into my legs which were bleeding. My sister also got a belting and I felt sorry for her, as she only came out with me because I wanted her to so she couldn't dob on me because she was part of it too.

After going out with my boyfriend for a while, I realised in Grade Ten that I could be pregnant. I was completely uneducated on any aspect of contraception, as sex was never discussed in our house. It was very much a taboo subject. I learned from the other girls in my circle of friends who all had their own boyfriends and I was doing nothing differently to any of them but it was me who fell pregnant. I resented that and asked myself why this had to happen to me and not to anyone else in my group of friends. I was very naïve about contraception, which is not surprising as I was still very young and had lived a cloistered life.

Of course, I told my boyfriend about my predicament. He tried to support me as best he could but he didn't have a clue what to do either. He was only 18 himself. I went to a doctor I had never been to before, as I didn't want my parents to know anything, and he confirmed my worst fears. I was pregnant. On that day and each monthly visit thereafter, I 'willed' that doctor to ask me if I wanted a termination because that is what I desperately wanted, but he never did, and I was too shy and embarrassed to ever ask for one. I kept going for regular monthly check-ups until, at around 20 weeks, he asked me if my parents knew about the pregnancy and I told him no. He said he thought it was time I told them. That day I left his surgery, on my own, and walked to a nearby park bench where I sat and cried. I felt sick in my stomach. I was in the depths of despair. I knew how devastated my parents would be and I knew how much trouble I would be in, as my father didn't even know I had a boyfriend. My mother knew but probably not the extent to which our relationship had developed. I didn't know what I was going to do and I was so scared and felt so alone and unprepared to deal with what was ahead of me.

I went home and the next morning I said I was not feeling well and I stayed at home with Mum. After the other kids had gone to school and Dad had left for work, I told my mother what had happened and I cried as I was so ashamed and embarrassed and guilt-ridden. She seemed genuinely shocked and scared. She said she needed to phone Dad to ask him to come home. She rang him and told him he needed to come home straight away. She didn't tell him why but said it was very important. I am assuming because of the seriousness of her tone he did not question her any further, and he came straight home from work. It was an agonising wait for me, and no doubt for Mum too, waiting for him to arrive home. It seemed like an eternity, like waiting for a tsunami to hit you while you are anchored in one spot, unable to run or move, frozen in the moment. Waiting for the tidal wave to hit. I felt sick.

When Dad came home it was Mum who broke the news to him and I was so pleased I didn't have to speak the words to him myself. The look on his face was one of utter shock and disbelief. He looked at me in disgust and disdain. The best thing I could do was bury my face in my hands and force myself to cry. I had already cried so much before this moment, it was now that I was feeling a sense of relief coming over me and, even though both of my parents were angry and trying to come to terms with what they were now confronted, I was starting to feel that I didn't have to carry this burden of weight and worry on my shoulders alone anymore. After a lot of talking and questioning and thinking about what to do next, but not coming up with any answers, my mother decided to ring her sister to ask for advice. After that call and more talking it was decided I would be sent away to another town to live with some people my aunt knew for the remainder of my pregnancy. I had brought great shame and I was being sent away to protect my family's name and my father's position and standing in the community. I was not to be seen by anyone over the next few months. This was a secret that no one outside of my family and my aunt's family would ever be told about, and it wasn't spoken about for nearly 30 years.

CHAPTER 3

YOU HAVE RUINED YOUR LIFE

At 15 years of age, I had to leave school and travel on a bus, on my own, from Mackay to Toowoomba, where my aunt lived. I had never done anything like this on my own before so it was very scary, but I was also relieved to be getting away from the pressure I had been living under at home, particularly when my father was drunk and began questioning me about the most intimate details of what had occurred. This was truly embarrassing for me and I knew that no matter what answer I gave it would be the wrong one and would just infuriate him more, which it did.

It was a shameful position to be in and I was also called all of the disgusting negative names that an unwed pregnant young woman would be called back in the 1970s. I was so ashamed; I just accepted these derogatory terms as my truth at that time. I had brought shame upon my family and I felt it acutely.

My experience of teenage pregnancy was not uncommon at all compared to others in my predicament back in the 1950s, 60s and 70s in Australia. During these years Australia had the highest rates of adoption in the country's history. There were really only three choices for girls who found themselves in this situation back in those days. It was either a shotgun wedding, and many girls were married at 16 and 17, or be sent away to adopt the baby out, or have an illegal backyard abortion, which was notoriously dangerous. I had no idea how or where such procedures would be acquired and I had no money anyway. For me, the decision was made by my parents: it was adoption, which also was in keeping with Catholic values. Unless you've been through this experience, no one can imagine the life-long impacts such a decision has on your life and that of the child born under these circumstances.

At the time of being young and pregnant, all the adults in my life were telling me I had ruined my life and my life was stuffed now, it was over, there was no coming back from this and every other message of "you've totally wrecked your life now" that one could imagine. I'd had this said to me in so many ways, so many times, by so many people and each time it was said to me, it jarred me to my core. I was indignant and determined to not accept that as my fate. I thought, how can my life be over when I am only 15? No, I won't let this happen to me. This can't be true and I won't accept it. I will not be defined by this experience for the rest of my life. I don't know where this resilience came from, probably my mother, who was herself a very strong woman, but I am so glad I did not accept what everyone was telling me as being my fate or things could have turned out very differently for me.

My aunt met me at the bus stop in Toowoomba. It was good to see her as she had always been a special aunty to me. She was my mother's younger sister who had lived with us in Brisbane with her husband and son while they were waiting to get a place of their own. So, I knew her well and she was very dear to me. She took me to meet the elderly couple who I would be living with for the next few months. They were friends of my aunt and were a lovely, elderly couple who I grew to fondly care for very much while I was staying with them. They had not had any children of their own. Both were retired and they warmly welcomed me into their modest little two-bedroomed cottage home, in the quiet western suburb of Newtown, Toowoomba, where they lived with their Fox Terrier, Penny.

I was placed with them to maintain the family secret of my pregnancy. My mother was from a large family spread throughout Queensland and many of them would pass through Toowoomba from time to time and when they did, they would stop off at my aunt's place for a visit. I could not be seen, so I could not live with her; however, my aunt and uncle were also very caring of me and looked after me very well during those few months of my life.

I had short visits to my aunt's place from time to time and she would take me to doctor's appointments, or to see the social worker at the public hospital, or for shopping together. She treated me very well and I have always been so appreciative of what my aunty did for me during such a very vulnerable time in my life.

The woman who I lived with had a good sense of humour. She was such a lovely person to me and would bake little treats for me to eat while telling me funny stories from her life, which always made me laugh. She did not judge me and always made me feel good about myself, which was unusual for me to experience at that time. She also taught me how to crochet and knit and sometimes we would do this together while we sat and talked. Often the old lady from across the street would also come over with her crocheting and she would join in our craft and conversation circle. They were very good to me and I remember these times with great fondness.

In saying that, I knew I needed to do more than knitting or crocheting, if those words, still ringing in my ears, "you've ruined your life", were not to become my reality. So, with the help of the hospital social worker I was enrolled into Correspondence School and started to receive Grade Ten learning materials each week. I became very regimented in my approach to my schooling each day and I applied myself as I had never done so before, getting very good grades in all of the subjects I studied. There was never any consideration given to having any tutoring to help me; it wouldn't have been possible anyway, as our family was not at all wealthy. Tutoring wasn't something I was familiar with as none of my friends or anyone I knew had ever had tutoring. I just needed to get on with it myself, do the study and apply myself to the task, so that is exactly what I did.

I had a small table with a chair set up in the corner of my bedroom where I studied each day. I would write out all of my assignments by hand, no computers back then, and I mailed them to the Correspondence School each week. I was really committed to my studies as I was determined to complete Grade Ten and get my Junior Certificate. I probably studied to the level of ability my teachers had always commented I was capable of, but never really putting my mind to the task. Whereas now, I was giving it my all. It is amazing what you can do when you have a clear goal in sight and you're determined to achieve it. This was a good lesson for me to learn. It is a focus I have always since maintained throughout my life, no matter what I strive to achieve.

I was fortunate my health remained good throughout the pregnancy so I could continue with my studies. I was due in September 1973 and I studied right up until I had to go to hospital to have the baby.

It was Sunday morning on September 9 that my carer called my aunty to say she thought I was in labour and should probably go to the hospital. I had started labour pains during the night but I didn't really know what they were. I just felt very restless and uncomfortable. My aunt came over and drove me to the hospital where I was admitted, examined and taken through to the labour ward. I was dressed in a white hospital-issued shift and put on the birthing table in the labour ward. The contractions were coming very strongly so I was given gas to inhale, which I breathed in deeply as that was the only form of pain relief available in those days. The labour wore on for many hours throughout the day and, from time to time, one of the nurses would check on me before leaving the room again. I was left alone in that room for most of the day. My aunt came in to see me at one point but I was drifting in and out of sleepiness due to the gas I'd inhaled. I knew she was there but I couldn't remember anything she said to me. I remember every time I did wake up due to the pain of another contraction, I would look at the large government-issued clock on the stark white wall at the end of my bed and wonder when this was ever going to be over. The contractions were strong and coming every few minutes and the pain was almost unbearable. It seemed to go on forever. Eventually, the nurses appeared again and the baby was born naturally, later that night. It was a boy and he was quickly whisked away from me. I didn't even get to see him. I heard him cry but I was exhausted and as I was being stitched up, I fell back into semi-consciousness from the effects of the gas.

I was later to learn that my aunty phoned my mother to let her know I'd had the baby and it was a boy. Apparently, my father was nearby to my mother at the time of the phone call and he knew it was about me, so he asked her if I was okay, to which she replied "yes". He said that was all he wanted to know and he walked away. He never knew whether I had given birth to a boy or a girl, not to his dying day. He did not want to know. Maybe it made it easier for him to cope with, knowing his first-born grandchild was being given away and he would never see or have anything to do with that child, ever.

Back in the maternity ward the next day, I was thankful to be in a room of my own and not have to mingle with the other mothers or see them cuddling their babies. I was given tablets to take to dry up my milk and other pain relief medications as I was fairly well messed up and could hardly sit down. Throughout my few days in that hospital I was spoken down to by the matron and all the nurses alike. I was made to feel very much like the little slut they all thought I was. I did have visits from my aunt and my carers and I received flowers from Mum and Dad, which were delivered to my room. It was a nice surprise and some indication of forgiveness too, I hoped.

After a couple of days recovering from an exhausting and traumatic birthing experience the matron brought in the adoption papers for me to sign. She explained to me that I must fill out the forms she was giving me and I must write that the baby's father's is 'UNKNOWN' because he was not there to sign the papers as well. So, not only was I being treated like a little slut by all of these nursing staff, now I had to confirm that in writing by stating on the form that the child's father was 'unknown'. I felt very affronted and I thought "I don't think so", but I didn't say that to her. I just listened to the instructions I was being given. Then she left the room and the papers just sat there. I didn't want to fill them out at all. I wanted to see my baby boy. I asked a nurse to see my baby but was told that would not be possible given he was to be put up for adoption. I thought about this for a while and then I asked the nursing staff again if I could see my baby. Again, they said I couldn't, so I said to them, "Then I am not going to sign the adoption forms until I do see him." To this the nurse said that she would speak to the doctor and see what he said.

Soon after that my aunt arrived to visit me. She had obviously been told of what I had said to the nurse and she began to talk to me about signing the adoption forms. I told her I didn't want to adopt the baby out but she went to great lengths to point out that I was not in a position to raise a child and my parents wanted me to adopt the baby out and every other reason why I needed to do this for the baby's future and not think about myself, not to be selfish but think of what is best for him. Still I stood my ground. This was a very distressing time for me. I was very torn between what my parents wanted and the maternal instincts within me to hold on to and raise my own child.

My aunt spoke to my parents to update them on what I had been saying about not wanting to adopt the baby out. My father asked my aunt to pass on the message to me that if I did not adopt the baby out, I was not welcome to come home. I was in a no-win situation and this was back in the years before there was any government parenting allowances or supported housing or accommodation for young mothers, as there now is. It would have been me with a baby and nowhere to live, with no means of supporting ourselves. What choice did I have? None.

The matron came and told me the doctor had agreed for me to see my baby. I was overjoyed that I would get to meet him at last. They brought him to me wrapped in a bunny rug. I held him and cradled him and stared into his perfect tiny red face and I tried to emblazon that adorable little face into my brain, so I would always remember what he looked like and I could, at least, carry that image with me always, in my memory. Then, after half an hour or so, they came and took him away from me. I cried and cried and cried. It was the deepest sadness I had ever felt and for many years that sadness never left me.

What has stayed with me from that experience was that as a 15-year-old, I stood my ground and insisted that I saw my son without anyone encouraging me or suggesting to me that I should do so. I did it of my own volition and I have always been proud that I stood up for myself and got to meet my tiny son at that time. To be so strong and to have done that, as a young girl, has given me great comfort over the many years that I did not know my son.

Soon afterwards, I completed the adoption papers, but I wrote the father's name on them, despite being told not to do so. I wanted the nursing staff to know that I did know who the father was and I was not the little tramp they thought I was. When the matron came back to collect the papers she took one look at them and told me I should not have written the father's name on the form and I needed to fill them out again, as she had instructed me, with the father's name written as 'UNKNOWN'. She tore the completed forms up in front of me and handed me more forms and said, "Now, do as you are told, and fill the forms out as you have been told to." Again, I was in a position where I had to comply, so I did what I was told to do, but I felt terrible having to do that, like a real little tramp.

I was told I had 30 days to change my mind about the adoption and I wish I had not been told that because every day for 30 days I thought about him and I wanted to change my mind and go and get him, but I knew I couldn't do that. It was 30 days of agony for me. When day 31 came around I knew that choice was taken away from me and there was nothing I could do now. It was done. There was no grief and loss counselling for me after this experience. I was simply returned to my carers' house by my aunt, where I was warmly greeted by them both, and by Penny too. It was a relief to be home from hospital and back with caring people who were kind to me and didn't look down their noses at me, but who looked after me and treated me with respect.

Soon after returning to my carers, I decided to resume my studies to complete my schooling. I spoke to my aunt and I was enrolled in Harristown State High School in Toowoomba for the last couple of months of the school year. I quickly made friends there and settled into my classes. I was unable to pick up two subjects which I had been studying previously because the school did not offer these subjects. I completed and gained a pass in Grade Ten by the end of 1973 and I was so pleased that I had completed my Junior Certificate. I felt a sense of accomplishment and relief that I had actually done it and somehow it meant I wasn't a failure; it was the first step in proving everyone wrong, that I had not ruined my life.

At the end of the school year my parents drove to Toowoomba to collect me. It was so good to see my mother again. I loved her dearly. She had written to me regularly while I was away and she would often put a $5 note in her letters to give me a little bit of spending money. I was very unsure of how my father would be towards me so my approach towards him was much more tentative. I waited for him to give me some indication of how he was going to be. I think we were pleased to see each other but reticent to be too welcoming at that first meeting after many months, especially given all that had happened between us before I left Mackay.

When it was time to leave to go home to Mackay, I said my goodbyes and gave hugs to my carers and to my aunt, all of whom had been so good to me over the past months. We got into the car, my mother, father and me, and we started to head off on the long drive north. My father said to me that I was to now put all of 'that' behind me. It didn't happen and none of us were to ever speak of it again, not ever, not to anyone. So, it never was, not even in our family. Not for many, many years at least. I didn't even know if my youngest sibling knew what had happened or why I went away for so long and he never asked me, so I assumed he didn't know and I never told him either.

CHAPTER 4

REVOLVING DOORS

It was good to be back in Mackay and see my friends again and try and get back some sense of normalcy in my life. I visited my best friends at their homes and spent time enjoying being with them again and talking about the latest fashions or what was in the latest *Dolly* magazine or catching up on what other friends had been doing while I was away. Just hanging out together and enjoying being in each other's company for the first time in a long while. It felt good and familiar and comfortable to me.

Instinctively, they seemed to know to not ask me too many questions about what happened while I was away; even though my closest friends knew why I had left, they were not intrusive with their questioning, which I was very thankful for. They seemed to understand I didn't want to talk about it, so they didn't ask, but talked instead about life in Mackay since I had been away. It was so good to be back with them again and start to pick up some of the threads of my life from the time before I was sent away. Although I knew, deep within myself, that I was a different person now.

I'm not really sure what my parents told others about why I went away. I don't think they told anyone other than my aunt and my mother's close friend who lived nearby. I think the official line was that I had been sent away to boarding school to finish Grade Ten. I did have a couple of girls ask me if I had gone away to have a baby, but because it was a taboo subject, never to be spoken of, I always denied it, although I don't believe I convinced them for one minute, but at least they didn't keep pressing me for more information.

Life back in Mackay moved into me joining a basketball team again with my friends and I started playing guitar again, as we had done previously. A few of us had learned and played guitar since the beginning of high school. I enjoyed playing music with my girlfriends at their homes but occasionally we were asked to play at other events in town. I remember we were asked to play at Michelmore's Christmas party one year. It was a large department store in Mackay with many divisions and a lot of staff, so a big hall was hired for the occasion. It was a bit of an honour to be asked to play, although one of my friend's father was the managing director, so maybe it wasn't so much of an honour and more of a favour to us. I didn't mind though, as we were each given new beauty cases as a gift, so we thought we were pretty cool. I was also asked to play guitar and sing solo at a friend's wedding and then asked to sing in a local pop band. I was the only girl and it was lots of fun singing and performing at teenage dances and other gigs in Mackay. I was there for vocals and played tambourine. I enjoyed practising with the guys and singing a lot of the popular songs back in the early to mid-'70s.

I loved music as I had learned to play piano in primary school, despite not owning or having access to a piano to practise on. When I got my callipers off during Grade Seven, I rode my bike, every week, to a little old lady's house in Maryborough, where she taught me piano for one hour at a cost of two shillings a lesson. I loved it but the only practice I got was when I went for lessons. I would have loved a piano to practise on at home but I knew that was not likely to happen so I just enjoyed my weekly piano lessons instead. Music has always played an important role in my life and it still does.

Back in those days I was in a hurry to grow up, get my driver's licence and enjoy life outside the strictness of my family life. That was what I dreamed of and longed for.

I had finished Grade Ten now and had my Junior Certificate, so it was time to get a job. My father said I could get a job with him at Telecom as a typist, so I started in January 1974. I was a terrible typist and that was back in the days when carbon paper was used to create copies of documents and making one mistake on the top sheet of paper meant having to fix it on two or three other sheets of paper underneath. Many of my finished documents had lots of fixed-up mistakes, and it looked like a dog's breakfast. I admit that myself. It was not good, but I did eventually improve over time with practice.

I do acknowledge my father gave me a good opportunity and he tolerated my poor typing skills which I was grateful for. I loved earning my own money and buying my own clothes and shoes and makeup and becoming more financially independent, although I was still living at home with Mum and Dad and my father still, at times, wanted to encroach into what I thought was women's business and none of his. I remember one time when we were driving to work together and he told me he thought my makeup was too heavy. Again, he was stepping over a line, I thought. If Mum had told me that I would have listened to her but I thought, what would Dad know about women's makeup?

My father's weekend drinking hadn't changed except that perhaps he had become more abusive and angrier than I had remembered before. He continued to abuse us all and was still at times physically abusive to anyone in the family who dared to express an opinion which differed from his. We were all empty-headed. My older brother was an "empty-headed, long-haired lout" and my mother, sister and I were all "empty-headed, dumb bitches". These were his most commonly used descriptors of us.

There were times when my older brother tried to protect my mother from another violent incident and on one particular occasion my brother ended up with a broken bone in his hand which had to be set in a plaster cast. My father later told him there'd be more where that came from if he tried anything like that again. My brother would have been about 17 at the time. My sister also experienced these distressing occasions but my younger brother seemed to be spared from my father's wrath, perhaps because he was the youngest child. I don't really know why he didn't cop it as much as the rest of us but this was how it was.

It always bewildered me that my father could carry on in his abusive drunken stupor every Friday evening, Saturday afternoon and evening, and then get up early on Sunday morning, as though nothing had happened, and tell us all to "get ready for church". I would look at him in disbelief at the ludicrous hypocrisy of even suggesting that to us. When we reminded him of what he had done and said the previous night he would tell us not to be so stupid, that he didn't do or say any of those things. It was like he was two completely different people in the one body, a real Dr Jekyll and Mr Hyde.

On another occasion, when he had been particularly abusive towards my mother, she and my younger sister had gone to stay at a neighbour's house. The neighbour had become a very good friend of Mum's, and thank goodness she was there too, as there were many times my mother would need to retreat to the safety of her house from my father's drunken and abusive rants.

Revolving Doors

My mother and sister had been at our neighbour's place for about four days at the time. I was still living at home, as I had to go to work each day with my father, so I had to see him every day anyway, no point in moving out as well. It was Sunday morning and my father said we were going to church and he told me to get ready to go. I said I wasn't going to church, as I was just too consumed with the total hypocrisy of the whole situation. I also thought, I know he is going to lose it with me, but if I am old enough to have a baby then I am old enough to know whether I want to go to church or not, and I didn't want to. So, again, I said, "I am not going to church." He grabbed my long blonde hair and flung me around, telling me to go and get dressed or he would dress me. I stood my ground and said I wasn't going to go to church. He then grabbed the flannelette nightie I was wearing, which had long sleeves and buttons down the front of it, and as he swung me around, he ripped two buttons off, again telling me to go and get dressed. I still said I wasn't going to go to church. He then said he was going to get his belt and when he came back, I'd better be dressed for church or I would cop the belt. When he went to get his belt, I took off. I ran up the street to the neighbour's house, where my mother and sister were. I quickly told Mum and the neighbour what had happened and I was told to go into one of the bedrooms and stay there. Next thing I heard my father's voice at the front door asking for me to come out. Our wonderful dear neighbour answered the door and she told Dad I was going to stay at her place and I wouldn't be coming out to go with him. He asked a couple more times for me to come out but each time he was told I was going to be staying there. He eventually turned around and went home. A little later we all saw him drive past the house on his way to Sunday Mass.

After all of this happened, while Dad was still at church, I went home and packed my things. I phoned a friend to give me a lift to the local girls' boarding house hostel, Cromer House. My mother knew where I had gone but we had agreed she would not tell him where I was because we both knew he would come looking for me. I moved into Cromer House and lived there for several months. My father went to the police and reported that I was missing and I had stolen a suitcase from him. He wanted me charged with stealing. The police apparently told him to go away. I found this out years later when my mother told me about it.

At this time in my life, I knew I couldn't work with my father any longer, so I immediately started to look for another job and I never did go back to my job at Telecom.

I went to the Commonwealth Employment Service, which was the only place to go to put your name down to look for employment back in the 1970s, and they immediately referred me for an administration officer's position with the South British and United Insurance Companies which operated out of the one office. I went for the interview, got the job, and became financially independent from my parents. I budgeted my money, paid my own bills, went to work each day, which I could easily walk to from where I was living, and I felt relieved I didn't have to put up with my father's stressful and abusive temperament any longer. I did feel sorry for my mother and sister though, as they were still stuck in that terrible situation.

My father did eventually find out where I was living and, on one occasion, he came to see me there. The boarding house supervisor, who knew why I had moved into the hostel, was watering the garden on that particular day when my father turned up at the front gate and asked to see me. She called me and I came out to see what she wanted when I saw my father at the end of the front path, standing near the front gate. I stood on the top step of the veranda. He said he wanted to talk to me and he tried to coax me out to his car, but I knew if I went to the car, he would take me home, so I didn't agree to that. The supervisor, who was facing me while watering the garden, whispered under her breath, without looking at me, "Don't go." She had nothing to worry about because I had no intention of going with him.

From that day onwards I did not see or speak to my father for the next two years. If ever he saw me in the street, he would cross the road and walk on the opposite footpath, but that was fine with me as I didn't want to talk to him either. I was very angry at him and no doubt he was angry with me too.

During those years, I lived a lot of life with a newly liberated feeling of freedom. I was rebellious and no longer had to be confined or restricted by my father's strict religious regime. I felt free; I became savvier about looking after myself and made sure I used contraception. I was never going to be in the same position again. I learned a lot from other girls in the hostel about how to look after myself too.

I got a second weekend job to earn more money. I worked as a shop assistant at fast food cafés and as a waitress at a restaurant in the evenings. I saved and budgeted my money well but I still managed to socialise with a lot of other young people. Life was good and I felt very independent. I went out, drank alcohol, began to see other boys, had myself a fantastic, fun time, but was dead set against doing drugs, despite them being offered to me at just about every party I went to. Drugs, particularly dope, were very commonplace at parties in the '70s. I think I was viewed as being a bit 'different' in this regard, but when the joints were being passed around, I had no trouble in passing it on without taking a puff. Maybe it was because I was not a smoker, even though I gave it a go like every other young person usually does at some point while growing up. I never took up smoking or allowed myself to feel pressured into doing drugs of any kind.

CHAPTER 5

TOADS AND PRINCES

After going out and socialising with friends at parties, eventually I met another guy who, not long afterwards, became my boyfriend. I never rekindled my relationship with the father of my son and I have never spoken to him since or even know of his whereabouts.

I felt very secure having a boyfriend who was older than me. He was 18 and a mechanic and had his own motorbike, a Honda 4. He later upgraded to a Kawasaki 750. I loved riding pillion on his bikes with him and we had some fantastic and fun times together. It was such a sense of freedom and fun being on his big motorbike with him. There was one occasion that my mother forbid me to ride on the back of his motorbike on a trip from Mackay to Brisbane. She had never forbidden me from doing anything before, so I knew she was deadly serious about this and, out of respect for her, I didn't go with him on that trip. She was also worried about my hip and the pain I would experience sitting on the back of a motorbike for such a long ride. My hip was starting to ache from time to time again.

I'd started taking painkillers more often to manage the pain, and she knew this too.

We did go to many bikie parties though, which were pretty wild affairs. These were places where I saw and heard some awfully disgusting things, but my boyfriend always kept me close to him and on a couple of occasions he told me we needed to get out of there quickly for my safety. I never questioned him. We just jumped on his bike and took off as fast as we could. Fortunately, nothing terrible ever happened to me at these parties, which was not the case for some others there. I'm so thankful for this because it could have gone terribly wrong so easily, I now realise.

My boyfriend was a very quiet person in public but he wasn't that way with me. He was very gentle and caring and we got on very well together and we talked about all sorts of things together. I felt very safe with him. We were together for a couple of years and during this time my mother bought me a little second-hand Ford Cortina which a friend of hers was selling. It was a good little car and at age 17, I had my own car and felt amazingly grown up. I had been through a lot in the last three years, so I did grow up quickly. I had to; I was looking after myself now and making all of my own decisions.

I was able to drive to my boyfriend's place to see him and I often stayed at his parents' house on the weekends. They lived on their sugar cane farm. His whole family were very quiet people and they didn't speak much at all at home either. It was a family trait that I became used to eventually. It was so different to what I was used to but I liked the absence of anger, abuse and tension in their house compared to my own family home. I became very fond of his mother and younger siblings during these years.

At age 17 my boyfriend and I decided to get engaged but because I was under 18 years of age, I had to get special permission to do this from the court. So, I completed a statutory declaration that I was living independently and was not financially dependent on my parents. It was submitted and approved, so we went ahead and got engaged. We had our engagement party in the backyard of his parents' house. My parents did not approve so they did not attend the party. Ironically, my new fiancé was the second cousin of the neighbour who had helped Mum out so many times in our street. So, she was at the engagement party, which was lovely for me to have her there.

Over the following months I was contacted by the Commonwealth Employment Service, as I had kept my name registered there for a public service job and they were contacting me to offer me a position in their own office, as a typist. I went for the interview and they gave me the job. I was so happy as I always had the goal of working in the public service, which I think my father had instilled in me. And here I was, now working for the Commonwealth Public Service. Before commencing I did have to go to Brisbane to sit an entrance test which I passed and then got accepted for the position. I was very happy as I settled into my new job, which also paid better than my insurance company job, so I felt I was moving up in the world, although I was starting at the very bottom of the ladder, in terms of public service positions, but that was fine with me because I was achieving another of my life's goals.

I moved out of the girls' boarding house into a large highset private home where I rented a single room and shared a small kitchenette with an Asian girl who rented another single room near mine. The rent was cheaper than the girls' hostel, being the main reason I moved out, but the downside was, I had to prepare my own meals, which I seldom did because I was often at my boyfriend's parents' house or we ate out.

Downstairs a married couple rented another larger room under the house. They were always very friendly towards me. It was a big

Queenslander house in the middle of town, where the owners, an elderly Maltese couple, lived and rented out their rooms for some additional income. They were kind to me but spoke only a little English and I didn't have a lot to do with them, just the pleasantries made in passing.

I had nowhere I could bring friends to because it was just a bedroom that I rented and they told me no boys were allowed there. Although as my room was at the front of the house, at the top of the front stairs, there was the occasional time when my boyfriend did come and visit me, but he never stayed long as I was terrified the landlady would find out and kick me out. Instead, I was always out and about, either at work during the week or socialising on the weekends, when not working at my second job. Life was good and I would often go and see my mum at the shop where she worked, as I couldn't go and see her at home with my father being there and us still not talking to each other.

As time went on, I started to talk to my fiancé about setting a date for our wedding. He always seemed evasive about doing this and after a few attempts to have this discussion with him, it dawned on me that maybe he was having second thoughts about marrying me, otherwise why would he not be happy to set a date for the wedding? Maybe he didn't really want to go ahead and get married to me? Then I started to ask myself, well, if he feels like that, do I really want to marry him? And the answer I eventually settled on was "No, I don't".

This was a sudden realisation to come to for me and one that I had to think through now that I had opened that Pandora's box. There was no going back, but there'd been an engagement party and we had all those presents given to us. What would people think? What would I do? Surely, I couldn't go ahead and marry someone who I realised I didn't want to marry because we'd announced our engagement publicly in the newspaper and had a party and accepted all the presents from family and friends, and what about his family? What would they think of me? What would my parents think? They'd have been right that I shouldn't have gotten engaged to him in the first place. I had a lot to think about.

After much soul searching my mind was made up and I broke off our relationship. He was shocked and begged me not to leave him but I'd made the decision and there was no turning back for me. Something had shifted in me and my decision was made.

He didn't give up trying to win me back though. He would wait outside my workplace and walk beside me to and from the post office or other places I had to go to for work errands. I asked him not to do that but he said it was a public footpath and he could walk on it if he wanted to. There was nothing I could do about it. This type of harassment went on for weeks before he finally realised that I was serious and I wasn't going back to him. That's when he became angry at me and began saying he wanted back all of the things he'd ever given me as gifts and he wanted his share of the engagement presents, which I thought was fair enough. So I packed up my car with everything he'd ever given me, including the engagement ring, a sewing machine he'd bought for me and half of the engagement presents, and took them all to where he was with his mates, at a local pub, which had big open doors onto the footpath, so he saw me coming. I left everything on the footpath for him to get home, on his motorbike, the best way he could. In retrospect, it was a little mean of me to do that, but he had been harassing me endlessly for weeks, and I'd had enough.

In the months that followed I spent more time with my sister who had become an apprentice hairdresser at a local salon. I started going there from time to time to get my hair done so I'd become friendly with the other hairdressers there too. There was one hairdresser in particular who said she was going to be moving out of her sister's place and was looking for a flat to rent and someone to share with. I said I would share with her if she would like, as we both got on well together, and this meant I could be in a place of my own and not just in a room of my own. She was really happy at the suggestion for us to share a flat so we found one fairly easily, signed up and moved in together. It was great and we never had a cross word with each other. She was a little older than me and a great cook who loved cooking, so we always ate well. We didn't have much furniture of our own and thankfully the flat was partially furnished with beds and a dining table, at least.

We made it comfortable and I remember we got a large, sturdy cardboard box, which we turned upside down and covered with some brightly coloured fabric, that became our TV stand. We bought some big cushions to sit on for the lounge room floor and the bedrooms and bathroom were upstairs. We had water plants growing out of little green Mateus wine bottles which were positioned on the end of every second step of the internal timber staircase, which was very much the common indoor décor in those days.

We made do with what we had and what we could afford, and it was perfectly fine for us. Every Saturday morning the landlord would come around for his $42.50 weekly rent. My contribution was half of that amount each week. How times have changed. We went out dancing at the clubs and pubs, including the Oriental Hotel which was the place to go in those days. We had lots of fun together. Sometimes there were other girlfriends who would join us on these outings; it was a fun time and we enjoyed ourselves while giving cheek to lots of guys and we did lots of flirting along the way. Those were the days!

As I was single during this time, and occasionally my ex-fiancé was still harassing me to go back to him, my mother thought she would intervene to prevent this from happening. She told me later she was worried I would go back to him. She had met a footy mate of my older brother and she thought he was nice and had a bit more life in him, much more suited to me. The first time she met him, he and my brother had had a few drinks after a footy game and they both ended up back at my mother's house where they were mucking around and being drunk and silly in a playful way. My brother's mate had picked up a broom and was pretending to play it like a guitar, while singing some drunken song. Apparently, it was very funny. A few days later my mother suggested to my brother that he should bring this guy over to meet me at my flat and this is exactly what happened in the weeks that followed.

My sister told me about him. She had met him through my older brother too and she told me he was a nice guy who owned his own car and he had a boat and he was also an only child, so he was pretty well off. She said he had given her a lift home recently. I always joked, in later years, that she went out with him before I did, which she dismissively denied every time.

Dutifully, my older brother brought him over to my flat and introduced him to me. His name was Gary and he worked at a local electrical spare parts business in Mackay. I found him to be such a friendly, outgoing and chatty guy. So different to what I had been used to with my previous boyfriend. We got on really well together, right from the start. He was really funny and made me laugh a lot. We had a similar sense of humour, so being with him was very light and uplifting for me. I thoroughly enjoyed being in his company with his quirky sense of humour.

He started sending me little messages at work which were funny and he'd asked me out to dinner and sent me flowers. We were getting on very well and started going out together. After a short while together I was asked to represent the Mackay Brothers Rugby

League Club, as their Miss Rugby League Contest entrant. That was the club that my brother and my now boyfriend played at, so what could I say? I agreed to do this and entered the competition which was nothing more than a beauty contest really, as I hadn't been asked to do any fundraising for the club. Every club had an entrant for this competition. I think there were about seven clubs in the competition in Mackay at the time. Each girl had to undergo an interview by a panel of judges and, at a special gala dinner, the winner was announced and to my surprise, I won it! This meant I was crowned and received a 'Miss Mackay Rugby League' sash. The next step in this competition meant I then had to travel to Townsville to enter the next phase of judging.

"Miss Mackay Rugby League 1975"

Toads and Princes

It was the Miss North Queensland Rugby League competition and my mother came with me. It was quite funny really because each girl had to stand in the back of a ute, wearing her sash, and on the side of the ute was a sign with each girl's name on it and where they were from. For some reason unknown to me, they displayed my middle name, Marie, and surname, and not my first name, so it wasn't even correct. All girls were driven around and around the sports reserve in Townsville, while the judges announced who we all were and where we were from, eventually announcing the winner. It wasn't me but that was perfectly fine. I think it was Miss Innisfail Rugby League who won the title that year, not that it matters as it is such a frivolous and silly exercise, as I came to realise in later years.

My mother and I stayed at a Townsville motel overnight and we were due to fly back to Mackay on an early flight in the morning but our alarm didn't go off and we missed our flight. We both woke up, looked at the time and panicked as we realised, we'd missed the plane. Then we had to sort out how to get home to Mackay. I think we caught the next flight. We laughed about that many times in later years.

The year was 1975. I remember it well as it was the time when Gough Whitlam was dismissed as prime minister which caused a great uproar in Australia at the time. I didn't fully understand what was going on as I hadn't taken much notice of politics up to that point in my life. However, I was certainly listening with interest to the views of all the adults around me at work who were talking about the controversy of Gough Whitlam's dismissal. It wasn't until years later that I came to realise the full gravity of that momentous point in Australian politics. It was also an important year for another reason that I recall. It was the year that colour television came into being for us and that was very exciting indeed. Such a nice change from the old black-and-white everything on TV.

The relationship with my new boyfriend and I couldn't have been going better and nor could I have been happier. He spent a lot of time at the flat with me and we both knew we had something very special going on between us. I had told him all about the adoption of my son which he was very accepting of, but I swore him to secrecy and asked that he not tell anyone ever, to which he agreed.

By this time, I was 18 years of age, having grown up quickly due to all I'd been through. So, when he, being 22 years of age, asked me to marry him after we'd been going out together for just four months, I was very thrilled to say "yes". We were both blissfully happy together. It was a lovely time of life for me and for us both.

Our friends thought we were crazy. They said we were both on the rebound, as he'd not long left a relationship with another girl before he met me and I'd not long left the relationship with my ex-fiancé. We did't care what they all said. His parents were lovely and very welcoming of me which was important given he was still living at home with them, so I would be seeing a lot of them over the coming weeks and months. My mother was happy because she had succeeded in her mission to divert me from returning to my ex-boyfriend and she genuinely liked my new fiancé and was happy for me.

We started setting some plans and goals for ourselves. We wanted to start saving to buy our own home so we each got ourselves second jobs again. I had left the other part-time second jobs I had by that time so was keen to look for another part-time job to help us save for our dream home. I learnt how to pull a beer and then became a barmaid at a local hotel in the evenings. After a while I moved from that job to start working on Saturday afternoons in the bar at the local race track each week. He had a job pencilling for a local bookmaker at the races every Saturday so we worked there together, saving as much money as we could towards a deposit for our first house. He also sold his boat to raise more funds which helped to raise the level of our savings.

To save more money, I asked if I could move back in with my parents, as my father had distanced himself from me and mostly left me alone now. He also seemed accepting of my new fiancé who did, in fact, quite nervously, ask my father for my hand in marriage to which my father agreed.

We had our engagement party in the backyard of my parents' house and it was a very happy occasion which was nice as there'd not been too many of these happy moments at my parents' home, in my recollection.

After another eight months of working hard and saving all that we could we had enough to put a deposit on a house, so we went to the bank to have a talk with them about how much we could borrow for a new home. They said with the deposit we had raised, we could purchase a house up to the value of $30,000 so we set about trying to find a house which we liked for under that value. It was hard and the areas we wanted to buy in, on the south side of the river, had real estate that was mostly over the $30,000 mark so we had to start to look a little further afield. This led us to look in the suburb of Andergrove which was still a fairly new-developing suburb on the outskirts of Mackay in 1976. We found a brand-new 'spec house' in Maple Drive which we could afford, a highset, three-bedroom home with a price tag of $28,500. The bank gave us the loan and we purchased our first house before we were married in May 1977. We had pretty much used up most of our finances and the wedding was yet to come.

I was the first of my siblings to get married. Despite our differences my father accepted his responsibility of paying for his daughter's wedding reception which he had to take out a loan to do. My husband's parents paid for the alcohol, as was the custom at the time. We married on May 21, 1977, one year after we had first met each other. I was 19 and Gary was 23 years of age.

"Our Wedding Day"

We scraped together enough money to buy some basic pieces of furniture for our new home—a bed, a lounge suite and a dining suite. My husband's parents paid for the carpet to be laid in the house which was great as we couldn't have afforded to do that. My mother gave us a second-hand fridge which she had. It had some rust on it but this was easily patched up with white contact to make it look passable. It worked, which was the main thing. We bought a little twin tub washing machine because it was cheap; we had all the basics we needed to get by with. It was our home and we were happy there together.

Before we even moved into our new home, we set off on the day after our wedding to start our honeymoon. I remember when we were driving out of Mackay, I thought how happy and lucky I was to have met such a wonderful man, but then it dawned on me that he might change now that we were married. I turned to him and said how happy I was, but I also said, "If you ever lay a hand on me, make no mistake, I will leave you." He looked at me in utter surprise, shock and disbelief at what he had just heard. He had never done anything to me to indicate he would be violent towards me but I also remembered my mother saying how wonderful my father was when they were going out together and when they first got married, before it all turned so bad.

Gary looked at me and promised me he would never do anything to hurt me and he has never been domestically violent towards me at any time throughout our entire marriage.

We honeymooned in Cairns and the Atherton Tablelands but after having to pay repairs for the car we were driving to replace a shattered windscreen and an exhaust pipe that fell off, we were left short of money for the rest of the honeymoon. We had packed a little two-person tent, mostly at the urging of others who said we'd really enjoy camping up there. I didn't think for one moment that we would actually use it, until these unexpected car expenses came along. We had enough money to stay a couple of nights in motels along the way but the rest of the time we camped in the tent. I remember setting the tent up in a caravan park in Cairns and it started to rain, heavily. It was one of those northern monsoonal types of rainfalls and it just kept pouring down. We sat in the middle of the tent, trying to not touch the sides of it to prevent the water coming through where we might have brushed it. We looked at each other sitting in that tent, in the middle of a torrential downpour, and I said I'd like to go home, to our brand-new home. We both agreed that's what we'd do so as soon as the rain stopped the next morning we packed up and drove back to Mackay, to start our new life together in our new home. Life was good.

CHAPTER 6

SPECK ON A MAP

After being married for about six months, the take-away food shop where my mother had worked for years was put on the market. My mother was very encouraging of us to consider buying the business. She said it was a good income earner, she knew it well, and she was willing to help us get started in the business. After all, the business traded on the food it sold and my mother was the cook there, so it was her efforts that really made this such a good little business.

Gary was very keen on purchasing the business and getting ahead as quickly as possible, so we approached the bank again and got the loan to buy the business. It was an exciting, but slightly scary time as we took a risk to give this a go, without having any previous experience as business owners.

As our financial backup insurance plan, we agreed I would remain in my job working at the Commonwealth Employment Service and bringing in a regular wage, until we were sure we could make a living out of this new business for ourselves.

For the next three years every morning Gary got up very early at 5.00 a.m. to go into the shop and put the chickens on the rotisserie to start cooking so they'd be ready when the doors opened at 7.00 a.m. every day. The shop sold take-away food—burgers, fish and chips, all sorts of home-made types of meals, small cakes and slices, and had a small grocery line. All cooked products were made by my mother. She was a very good cook, I always thought, and judging by the trade of the business for her cooked items, many others thought so too. She worked very hard, which was nothing new to her, she'd worked hard all her life. She was a wonderful role model for me and my siblings.

The shop was a seven-day-a-week business and was open for 12 hours each day. It was a long, hard slog. I worked in the shop after my day job, on some weekdays, and on weekends. We didn't have a lot of time away from the shop together but I didn't mind initially, as I could see this as the way we would get ahead financially, or so I thought.

After working hard for the first two and a half years of our marriage we decided to try for a baby of our own, which I desperately wanted. I never stopped thinking about my other child and wondering where he was and whether he was safe and happy and being well cared for, but I never spoke about this to anyone, not even to Gary. It became the topic we just knew to never speak about, not even to each other, so we didn't.

It was only a short time after deciding to try for a baby that I realised I was pregnant. We were so happy and the pregnancy went really well and I didn't have any health concerns relating to my pregnancy. As I gained weight though, my hip began to ache more than it had been aching, although the pain of my hip aching had become just a normal part of my daily life by this time. Almost every day I was taking painkillers to get through the day.

The pregnancy progressed well and in January of 1980, our first child, a boy whom we named Ross, was born. He was the apple of our eye and of his grandparents' eyes as well. He was the first grandchild for them all. Well, the first that my parents had met, that was. I loved being a mother and Gary loved being a dad. I was 21 years old by this time and I took 12 months maternity leave from the Commonwealth Employment Service where I was still employed, so I could be a full-time mother for the first time. That year went by so fast and I loved watching Ross grow and meet all his developmental milestones. We visited the child and maternal health nurse every week for a weigh-in and check-ups. I really didn't want to have to go back to work, but I did, as we were still trying to get ahead financially. I arranged child care for Ross and returned to full-time work after my maternity leave.

Like every other working parent, my routine became a rush of getting up early, getting myself and Ross breakfast and ready for the day ahead, then getting out of the door in time to get him to day care and myself to work on time. Gary left very early every morning as usual, so he didn't get to be a part of this morning routine rush to get out the door. Ross was asleep when Gary left very early each morning and asleep by the time he got home around 9.00 p.m. each night. To ensure they had some time together, at the end of my work day, I would collect Ross from day care and take him to the shop so he and his father could spend a little time together. It could only be a short time though, as I had to travel home, which was on the north side of the river, on the other side of town, and get Ross fed and bathed and into bed before it got too late and he got tired and cranky. It was always a rush to do this but it was worth it for Gary and Ross to have some special time together.

All this running around was taking its toll on my hip which gradually continued to deteriorate and after numerous visits to the doctors and specialists and being prescribed anti-inflammatories, painkillers and even having a cortisone injection directly into the hip joint to try and manage the pain, it had come to the point where the orthopaedic specialist said there was no further treatment available and the only option was to have a total hip replacement. He was reluctant to do it though as I was only 22 at the time and he didn't like to perform this surgery on young people but he acknowledged it was probably necessary to enable me to live a life free of pain and to function and have a better quality of life, particularly with a young family to care for now.

I was booked in for hip replacement surgery which was undertaken in November 1981. I took sick leave from my job for the time off. It was a big operation and I got quite sick afterwards and lost a lot of weight. I wasn't carrying much weight to begin with so I got quite thin. Eventually, after weeks of physiotherapy and help from my family I began to recover and was walking again and, for the first time in years, I was pain free, which was wonderful. It was nevertheless still a challenging time because of having to care for and run around after a young toddler combined with the pressures on Gary of running the business. My mother and his parents were a great help to us during this time.

After owning the business for three and a half years I had had enough of the long hours, of never seeing Gary and when I did, he was dog tired, and I was concerned about Ross and Gary not having much time together. This, together with Gary's propensity towards gambling on the horses, which I'd come to learn was more than just a little flutter now and then, meant we were not realising our dreams of getting ahead as much as I had hoped we would by then. I wanted to sell the business and have a normal family life.

Gary agreed to sell the business, so we put it on the market and waited to see if we got any interest. During this time, the man who had delivered milk to the shop every day for years, who we'd come to know very well, asked Gary what he was going to do once the shop sold. We didn't really have any idea of what he might do. So, he asked if we might be interested in moving to Dysart to take up the milk run there.

Dysart is a small speck on the map, it is a mining town, population of about 2,500 people at the time, situated approximately 250 kilometres to the south west of Mackay. It was a township specifically constructed to house the coal mining workforce and their families back in the early 1970s. Dysart supported the workforce for two coal mines situated on the outskirts of the township: Saraji and Norwich Park. The milk run included daily household milk deliveries and shop deliveries (there were two supermarkets in the town and a couple of service stations, cafes and a Chinese restaurant). There were also deliveries to the mine site's mess, or workforce dining area, for the predominantly male employees who lived at the mine site. There was a house provided which meant we could rent out our home in Mackay, so it seemed like a good move to make for our family at the time. Although, it meant I would have to leave my job at the Commonwealth Employment Service which was hard to do as it was my dream public service job. However, I knew we wanted to have more children so I'd have to leave at some point and this seemed to be too good an opportunity to pass up. The shop sold for the price we wanted for it so I gave up my job and we packed up and moved out to Dysart at the end of 1981 to start the next phase of our life together.

Dysart was a great place for men. It was a man's town. The men played all types of sports and they mostly worked hard, played hard, and drank hard. Gary played squash and football and enjoyed all of the masculine culture that permeated the township. He loved it there. Why wouldn't he?

The workforce comprised mostly men and there were very few jobs for women there, apart from a few admin positions in the mines;

there were also some retail jobs in the local shops but all jobs were quickly snapped up by women whenever a vacancy occurred. There was hardly any staff turnover to create employment opportunities for other women wanting to work in the town. As a consequence, for the majority of women, there was a culture of morning teas, playgroups, playing sport or doing handicrafts, and that was about the limit of the range of activities available for women in Dysart at that time. It was a young township, hardly any grandparents lived there, and there were a lot of young mums with young children in the town, similar to myself.

After moving to Dysart, where I had some relatives living who introduced me to other women in the town, I started doing the rounds of playgroups and morning teas at other women's homes. I quickly realised these were little more than town gossip sessions and I didn't want to be a part of that at all. So, as I couldn't play sport because of my hip, I turned my attention to learning all manner of arts and crafts. I joined the local craft club where I met many lovely women who were very talented in their respective crafts. I was very curious to learn many more crafts so I went to every lesson being offered that I could.

I have often reflected on this time and recounted with a smile that I think I learned every handicraft known to humankind while in Dysart. I could already crochet and knit so I went on to learn how to do patchwork, sewing, tatting, embroidery, lamp shade making, tissue box covering, oil painting, calligraphy, pottery and ceramics. I even went to Brisbane to train and qualify to teach ceramics with another friend in Dysart. Together, we held ceramic classes and lessons under her highset house for several years. There seemed to be a never-ending stream of women who wanted to learn this artform.

My friend and I both owned ceramic casts so we mixed and poured our own greenware and we purchased ceramic glazes to use and sell to women attending classes. We both owned our own kilns and we fired pieces for ourselves which we sold through the craft shop or gave to family members as gifts. We also fired pieces of ceramics for women who attended our classes. I enjoyed the creativity of teaching and creating these ceramic pieces for the few years we did this together. We didn't really make any money out of it because anything we earned, we put back into purchasing more products or upgrading our kilns but we really enjoyed these activities together and it kept us busy doing something we both enjoyed very much.

Not content with mastering ceramics I wanted to learn more about pottery so I undertook several classes and learned how to throw a pot, use a wheel and fire pottery which allowed for many more firing and pottery finishing variations than firing ceramics alone could achieve. I enjoyed learning all of these arts and crafts but after a while, I knew I could do them anytime I wanted to, so the challenge was no longer there for me. I started to look for other things to do. Eventually, I bought a heavy, old, second-hand upright Wurlitzer piano and I found a woman in town who taught piano. Before long I was back learning piano again and I loved it. I wasn't very good at it but I loved it. I found it very therapeutic and enjoyable and in trying to read the sheet music and practising the notes and melodies, mostly classical, I could lose myself in the music for hours.

I always kept an eye out for any employment opportunities while in Dysart and eventually a job came up for a part-time teacher aide at the local high school so I applied for the position and got it, which I was thrilled about. I was very happy to be back working again. Ross went to the local day care and I worked at the high school for about 20 hours per week. I enjoyed meeting the teachers and making friends with them, some of whom I am still friends with to this very day. The work consisted of preparing exercise sheets on an old spirit Gestetner printing machine for their classes or printing out test papers or anything else they needed to assist them in preparations for their classes. I worked in this job for about one year as during this time I became pregnant with our second son, Brad, which we were thrilled about. After having Brad, I did not return to the job at the school.

One of the teachers I had become friends with was also pregnant at the same time. We both ended up in the maternity hospital together in Mackay, having had our babies two days apart in February 1983. We became good friends and would often spend time at each other's homes after our babies were born, swapping stories about our children's progress or just catching up, as friends do.

After almost a year of caring for our two boys, Gary and I knew we both wanted more children and we hoped for a little girl to join our growing family so we decided not to wait any longer but to try and have another child as soon as possible to make up our family. Not long after we had made that decision, when Brad was about one year old, I found out I was pregnant again. This time though, I thought I'd had a miscarriage. I went to the doctor and told him what had happened and he said it was probably a blighted ovum, which I'd never heard of before, so I went and looked it up and it simply meant a miscarriage at a very early stage. He undertook a urine test in the surgery which was negative, so he thought that is surely what must have happened but he still suggested I have a blood test, to be sure.

He sent the blood test away and said he would be in touch again when he got the results back. I thought nothing more of it until I got a phone call from the doctor. He explained that the blood test had come back positive and said I should come back to see him as soon as possible. I made an appointment and saw him. He wrote me a referral to have an ultrasound to see what was going on for me.

The results of the ultrasound came back and clearly showed two sacs: one sac could clearly be seen to have an outline only, and within it, it was completely black, whereas the other sac showed an outline with a lot of static imagery contained within it. The doctor explained that I had been pregnant with twins and I had apparently lost one very early in the pregnancy, too early even to determine whether it was male or female, and the other sac contained a viable foetus. That foetus grew to become a gorgeous, healthy baby girl who was born in November 1984. Our family was complete when Heather entered the world.

"Heather, Anne, Ross, Gary and Brad – our Family"

While these early years in Dysart were in many ways very good years and we made a lot of lifelong friends from our time there, it was, at times, also very difficult for me, because Gary was very much involved in playing football, enjoying the mateship and drinking culture, and he was often away from the home leaving me to bear much of the parenting and child-care responsibility. He was also still gambling too much which was a constant source of tension between us. I became very resentful of his seemingly happy-go-lucky life while I was left to be the responsible main carer for our children. I became increasingly upset and unhappy.

After Heather was born, I had hoped that Gary's ways of being out with the boys would change, as he had promised me it would. However, his fun times with the boys didn't change and I soon sank into a dark post-natal depression. During this time, I had thought about ending my life, many times, and I had planned how I would do it. The only thing that stopped me was knowing that my children would grow up without a mother and I couldn't do that to them.

I was in a very dark place and I knew I needed help. I rang and arranged to meet with the local hospital social worker. I saw her a few times and she was wonderful as she was the one person I could talk to and tell how I was really feeling. She helped me enormously and with her skilful listening and therapeutic counselling sessions, she managed to eventually help to bring me out from the dark hole I was in and back to be more like my normal self. I have never forgotten that social worker or what she did for me. I am eternally grateful to her.

It was a busy time during these years and we crammed a lot into our life in Dysart and after our family was complete, we knew we didn't want any more children. I came to realise that the daily grind of looking after children, washing, cooking, cleaning and all the other household daily duties were going to be my lot in life, and I couldn't accept that my role was to be available 'to do' everything for everyone else, and nothing more than that.

I remember thinking, there has to be more in life than this, surely? I was only 26 and I thought I'd go crazy if this was what I would be doing for the rest of my life. I started to think about what I might want to do when Heather started school and then all the children would be at school. What would I do then? After working at the Commonwealth Employment Service and seeing many older women come to register for employment after their marriages had broken down, usually after many years of caring for and giving to their families, I realised they were really only employable in positions such as domestics, or housemaids, or kitchenhands, or cleaners. I knew none of those were for me. I knew I had to train myself so I was never financially dependent upon anyone else and I could contribute as much as possible to my family to ensure the children had a good education and we could have a good quality of life together.

I started thinking about what it was that I might train myself to do and I recall, as I was hanging nappies out at the clothesline, I asked myself a series of questions, like "what am I good at?" and "what do I like doing?" and "what am I not good at?" and "what don't I like doing?" The answers to these questions helped me to narrow down the direction I should head in. I liked people and thought I got on well with most people. In jobs I'd had I'd been complimented on my people and communication skills, so I thought that might be a good direction to go in, something working with people. I also thought about what I wasn't good at and that was clearly maths and science. I had never been good at those subjects in school and the thumping by the Irish nun in my Grade Six maths class popped into my mind to confirm I was not good at maths.

I pondered these thoughts for some months and during this time another part-time position became available as the local Dysart TAFE Coordinator. The woman who had done this job for years was leaving and it was advertised. I quickly applied for the position which I could do from home. The job consisted of basically finding out what types of hobby and recreational TAFE courses people wanted to do, then finding someone who could teach in that particular area, then matching them all up with each other so the course could go ahead. I also completed the enrolment paperwork, found the venues, made sure the trainers got paid and basically did all of the organisational side of things. It could've been any type of course at all that I might organise, as wide as the imagination. Some of the courses I arranged were pottery, calligraphy, and one time it was a farrier's course. Now, that one stumped me because I had a man who contacted me and asked if I could arrange a farrier's course. I said "I'm sure I can, but I don't know what it is" and I asked if he could explain it to me. He said it's horse shoeing, so I learned something new that day. Anyway, I got on and organised that course with one of the local stockmen teaching the horse owners who wanted to learn this skill. It was always very interesting and it was a great way to meet new people who I otherwise wouldn't have had a chance to meet, so I enjoyed it greatly.

The TAFE liaison contact, a man called Gordon, visited me every couple of months, travelling from Mackay to Dysart for a meeting with me. Over a cup of tea at my kitchen table he would ask how things were going with the courses and we would have a good chat about it all. During one of these chats I told him of my desire to train myself to do something when the children were all at school.

I mentioned that I had been thinking, for some time, that I should train in an area of working with people and I had thought social work would be a good profession for me but as I'd only completed Grade Ten at school I didn't believe I was eligible to study at university level.

He asked me if I knew about mature-aged entry to university, of which I knew nothing about, and he went on to tell me about how it was possible to study at university even without having completed Grade Twelve, as it was work and life experience as well as education that was taken into account when applying. I was very interested to hear more about what he was saying, as I saw a possibility of this being the way I should go, as far as future training for myself.

Gordon told me of a course that could be completed by distance education and once completed it could become a stepping stone to undertaking a social work degree. Gordon said the course was offered by James Cook University and it was an Associate Diploma of Community Welfare which could be completed in four years part time or two years full time. He gave me the name and contact details of the person I needed to speak to at James Cook University and he gave me all of the information I needed to know which then set me off in a whole new direction, that would eventually change my life forever.

Never underestimate the wonderfully unexpected opportunities that having a chat to one person may create in your life. That was the lesson I took from my chat over a cuppa with Gordon, a man to whom I am so grateful for the information he gave me that day and the way in which it then positively and irreversibly influenced my life.

CHAPTER 7

WORLD OF POSSIBILITIES

I was familiar with studying by distance education. I had done this before when I studied Grade Ten subjects by correspondence while in Toowoomba. I was enrolled in the Associate Diploma of Community Welfare with James Cook University in 1987. My study materials arrived and it all looked like a foreign language to me. After initially panicking and wondering what I had gotten myself into, I started having phone link-ups with the lecturers and other students, who I found out were all feeling much the same as me. Over time, as I read the study materials and participated in the phone tutorials and made connections with other students who were great supports to me and each other, I started to get into a type of routine with it all. It didn't happen quickly and the entire first year was a struggle as I learned to write as expected at university level. Feedback from assignments I'd handed in from the lecturers was extremely helpful in teaching me how to write to an academic standard.

Attending residentials on campus at university opened up a whole new world to me. I remember attending my first residential. It was on the Townsville Western Campus at James Cook University. I recall thinking I should pinch myself because surely it couldn't be true that I was really at university, enrolled in a university course? Wasn't I just an empty-headed, dumb bitch? What was I doing here? Yet, here I was and I was beside myself with excitement and beaming with self-pride.

I remember the Head of the School at the time addressing the whole group of students who had travelled from far and wide to attend this first residential and I will always remember his words to us all. After welcoming us and reminding us of how fortunate we were to have made the cut and be accepted into the course he went on to say that the usual attrition rate was something like 30% of students who commence tertiary study drop out after, or during, the first year. Then he reminded us that for each one of us who was accepted into the course, there was someone else who missed out. The significance of this really hit me hard. I felt such a weight of responsibility that I had kept someone else out of doing this course. I remember pledging to myself that day that I would not be one of the 30% of students who dropped out. I was there till the end and with resolute determination, I thought to myself, I *will* complete this course.

During the next four years I had the full support of Gary who, each night after dinner, would take the children into the lounge room to watch TV while I retreated to my desk, in the corner of our bedroom, where I studied each night, routinely. If the children came in to see me, I would give them a hug and a kiss and have a little chat to them, and then tell them to go back out to Daddy, which they did. For four years this was my religious routine, except for weekends when I studied whenever I could, usually when the kids were having a nap or outside playing in the backyard.

Initially, I think Gary assumed that studying was just my latest interest and eventually I would get sick of it and move on to something else, as I had done with all of the other craft and music interests I had taken up. However, for me, this was more than just a passing interest. I was loving everything I was learning. It was so different to anything I had ever done before and the new information I was learning was developing my intellect and challenging my beliefs and values at the same time. It was intrinsically interesting, extending my knowledge and I was hungry to learn more.

There were many times I'd had discussions with Gary about what I was learning and we'd had many conversations, arguments and debates over the new concepts, theories and views I was learning about and attempting to explain to him. His beliefs and values were also being challenged during these discussions as much as mine were and I don't think he liked that I was learning these new ideas.

I think he thought I was moving away from him, that a gulf was forming between us, in our belief systems, and I felt it too. We were growing apart and we both realised it. He became particularly angry during one argument about me studying and he picked up and tore a library book in half, down the spine of the book. I was horrified as it was a library book which had to be returned to the university library. This was an indication that he was not coping with the fear that he was losing me to another world, which he wasn't a part of.

After that incident, I made a decision that I needed to consciously work to reassure him that I loved him and studying at university did not mean I was growing away from him, although I was learning a lot of new information which he wasn't learning. I made a decision: if we were to remain together he needed to be engaged in what I was learning as much as I was, so I always discussed my study materials with him and, even though it often created more debates and arguments, he was and still is a person who will listen and consider alternative perspectives. Over time his views, values and beliefs have changed as much as mine have and we were very okay with that but it did take years of working together and acknowledging we wanted to be together, so we had to work on it together, but it was worth working for.

After my first year of study I was receiving subject results at credit and distinction levels which I was very happy about. A position had become available in Dysart as a Community Development Worker and as the committee knew I was studying Community Welfare and they'd advertised and couldn't get any suitable applicants, they asked if I would be interested in the full-time position. I said I was interested but I hadn't yet completed my course. They were not put off by this and offered me the job anyway, which I accepted. So now I was working full time, had three young children and a husband, and was studying part time. Life was busy but very rewarding.

About every four weeks or so, for all the years we lived in Dysart, we would travel to Mackay to visit family, go shopping, for doctors' visits, or just to have a break away from Dysart and see the ocean again. During these trips I would often stay at my parents' place with the kids, whom my father adored. He was always so much better with little children than he was with teenagers. He always went shopping before our trips to Mackay to ensure there was a little 'surprise' gift in the bottom of his cupboard for the children to find and delight over, which also brought him great happiness; that is a lovely memory I have of my father during those trips.

As an adult and a mother of three children I sometimes tried to talk to my father and I always tried to work him out but I never really could. He was not someone you could have a conversation with if your view happened to differ from his. You were always wrong and he was always right, so instead of not getting on with him, I just kept my views to myself for the sake of keeping peace.

World of Possibilities

My parents still lived together under the same roof but their marriage had long been over for many years. Yet, strangely, they still cared for each other and I could see that. I had asked each of them at different times when I was alone with them why they didn't separate and have some peace in their lives. My mother said my father would die if she wasn't there to cook for him, as he was a diabetic and needed to have a special diet and food made for him. And my father, still a die-hard Catholic, said he would never leave Mum because he'd taken vows at his marriage which he would not break as it was for 'better or worse', then he joked it just happened to be for worse. They stayed together until his death in December 1987.

This was the same year I had started to undertake my studies with James Cook University. My father could never understand why I was studying when my path was clearly already set in stone, as a wife and mother of three children. No matter how much I tried to explain to him my reasons for wanting to study, I don't think he ever understood why I would want to do it.

I got my subject results in November that year, so I was able to share with my parents the good news that I had achieved distinctions in some of my subjects. My mother was always encouraging and commented on how good that was and my father was interested in what I had told him and he asked me some questions about the subjects I had studied and how I found studying and he actually seemed to be proud of me. It was very satisfying to show him how I could achieve at university level of study and I felt a sense of accomplishment and pride in myself. I was also very happy that my father was impressed too.

It was not long after this discussion with my father that I returned to Dysart with the children, when in early December I received a phone call in the evening from my mother. The police had been at her door, telling her that my father had been found dead on the footpath outside a motel on Nebo Road. Apparently, he'd been walking home from the local bowls club, where he was the treasurer on the committee, and he'd suffered a massive heart attack and died there on the spot, despite a passing doctor stopping to render first aid; it was too late, he was gone. I couldn't believe what I was hearing from my mother. We ran around, packing bags, and collecting children, and we made a rushed trip from Dysart to Mackay to be with my mother.

I was 29 at the time and the shock of what had happened meant my mother was still trying to come to terms with my father's sudden and unexpected death. He was only 61 years old. My older brother was in Western Australia at the time and my younger sister and brother were both in Mackay but they were in shock too. Therefore, the responsibility for making all of the arrangements and decisions for my father's funeral fell mostly on me and I felt it acutely.

I'd come to realise, much later, that I had always held out hope of my father and I reconciling and understanding each other, but sadly that was never to be. Although, the tumultuous years of my adolescence had long passed and I'd learned better how to get on with him and not challenge him. For the most part that had worked much better for us over the latter years of his life.

After my father's death, I began questioning many things in life. Like, is there a God? What do I believe? I had turned my back on religion years earlier because of my life experiences and the hypocrisy I'd witnessed by many so-called 'good Catholics', including my father, but I'd been enculturated within Catholicism all my life. So, I was at a crossroads. This was the time I needed to make a decision about whether I believed in God or not because if I didn't then my father was gone and that was the complete end to life which was too painful for me to contemplate or accept then, so I started to turn back to religion, in a big way. I returned to regularly going to church and recommitting myself to the Catholic faith. I found it very comforting to do this and it helped me through the first year of grieving after my father's passing and trying to make sense of it all. Although, it did not last, as time would tell.

The months after my father's death was a time for deep soul searching about many things and I found that I was also questioning why I was even studying, despite the fact that I enjoyed it so much to that point. The answer I came up with was that I was studying to prove to my father that I could do it and to make him proud of me. That my life was not ruined or over from a mistake I had made as a teenager. I needed to prove him and everyone else wrong, but now he was gone. So why was I doing it now? Why would I continue to study now? Eventually, I realised and came to accept that now, I was doing it for myself, not for anyone else but me.

There was a deep sense of acceptance in reaching that conclusion and it gave me a renewed sense of determination and drive to keep going and prove to myself that I could study at university level and I could complete the course, which I eventually did at the end of 1990. I graduated with an Associate Diploma in Community Welfare and I couldn't have been prouder of myself for sticking with it and completing this qualification. It was such a sense of accomplishment and Gary, our children, my mother and siblings were all so proud of me too, which was just wonderful. We all travelled to Townsville from Dysart for the graduation and there were lots of photos taken of me with my family and the new friends I had made during the course of studying. It was a very happy day for us all.

I had come to learn how to study at tertiary level now and I had learned so much and realised there was so much more to know and learn about. I had always wanted to use the first course I'd studied as a stepping stone to undertaking study to complete a Bachelor of Social Work degree. That was my dream and my goal now. I searched every university in Australia to try and find anywhere that I could complete a social work degree by distance education but I couldn't find anywhere that offered it. Then I turned my attention to New Zealand to see if there was a university there through which I could undertake distance education to complete the social work degree, but there was nowhere that offered this degree by distance education in 1990 in either New Zealand or Australia.

I knew if this was going to happen, I would need to go to a university and study full time. As James Cook University would grant me full credit for the course I'd completed with them, from a social work degree, it was Townsville I knew I needed to go to, to further my education.

Gary and I spoke about relocating to Townsville. We'd lived in Dysart for nine years by this time and that is a long time in a small town and we also knew we wanted to be living in a larger town by the time our children reached high school to ensure they had as many opportunities available to them as possible. We agreed we'd move to Townsville so I could go to James Cook University to study social work full time and the children would have better educational opportunities as well.

In preparation for this relocation we took a trip to Townsville one weekend and looked around at properties in close proximity to the university, the schools and the shopping centres. We found a four-bedroomed house in the suburb of Cranbrook. It had an in-ground swimming pool, such a luxury for us who'd lived in a coal mining town for the last nine years, and we were sold. We signed a contract that weekend before returning to Dysart. At least we'd have a house to live in when we moved to Townsville, even if we didn't have jobs to go to.

World of Possibilities

On returning to Dysart we told our friends about our sudden purchase of a house and of our decision to move to Townsville so I could continue my studies at university. Some of our closest friends were happy for us but sorry we would be leaving Dysart, but many people in the town thought we were crazy, for a couple of reasons. The first reason was that my husband was following me, a woman, to do what I wanted to do, which was unheard of at the time, at least amongst the population of Dysart, which was such a masculinist and patriarchally organised community. The second reason was that we were leaving a perfectly good business to move to another city where neither of us had jobs to go to, with three young children. We didn't listen to them. We took a leap of faith and were confident we would find jobs in Townsville to support our family, which is exactly what we did.

After Christmas of 1990 we packed up our family and with three kids all looking out the back window of the car crying their eyes out, leaving their friends, and asking why we had to leave, as we drove away from Dysart for the last time, I felt terrible. It was me who we were doing this for and I was hoping they would understand one day, why I needed to do this to create a better life for us all in the long run. Gary was very supportive and accepting of this new adventure and next step in our life together.

It wasn't long after settling into our new home in Townsville and the kids were enrolled into their new schools that we both found work. Gary worked in a warehouse for QRX and, although I was enrolled as a full-time social work student, I found part-time work in the evenings as a youth support worker at a nearby shelter for homeless young women, operated by the Uniting Church at the time. So, we had an income and we had a home and our new life was beginning in Townsville.

I loved everything about being at university. I loved the feel and look of the campus. I loved just being on the campus with its beautiful large gum trees and stretching lawns and the creek that runs through the main campus, over which was a small footbridge which had to be traversed to get to the huge concrete library. I loved the academics who were all so welcoming and encouraging of me in my studies. I felt at home there, like it was where I should be. It felt so right for me. I loved the lectures and the tutorials and what I was learning and the lengthy intellectual discussions over coffee with other students in the refectory after lectures. There wasn't anything I didn't love about being at university, including the fact I made such good, lifelong friends. I'd found my place and myself at university.

I passed all of my course subjects, getting good grades, and I was even awarded a scholarship in the form of a HECS (Higher Education Contribution Scheme) exemption for one year, based on my overall grade point average. I thought it was a mistake when they told me I'd won this at first. I said I hadn't even applied for a scholarship and there must be a mistake but they informed me that the scholarships were awarded based on grades and as my grades were very good, I was awarded this scholarship. Imagine how excited I was? It meant I'd done so well with my grades that I didn't have to pay university fees for one year. That was huge to me!

Life in Townsville was good but it was 1991 when housing interest rates were 19% and we had the costs of a second house in Mackay which was still being rented and which we eventually sold. Gary's job didn't pay so well and I was on part-time wages. We were paying for private school fees for three children and university was expensive so, financially, it was a tough time for our family in Townsville to make ends meet. Gary wanted to borrow to buy another business to get out of his job and earn more. So, he looked around and found a green waste collection business which came with a big, old, orange-coloured garbage truck, with a hydraulic lifter at the rear of it.

World of Possibilities

I was against the idea from the outset but he was convinced it would be a good move to make so, despite my reservations, we went ahead and bought this business. It was hard, heavy, and hot work for him in Townsville, particularly during the summer months and when it rained. He lost a lot of weight while doing that job. It was physically demanding work moving those lawn clipping and green waste bags when they were wet, even with the use of a trolly. The boys were old enough by now to go with him and help him during school holidays or on weekends but it was a tough job for them all. The big old truck kept breaking down and Gary, not being a mechanic or mechanically minded, needed to get it repaired often which meant the profits of the business were quickly gobbled up with paying for truck expenses. These years in Townsville were probably the most financially stressful time of our lives but somehow, we managed to eventually get through it all okay.

It was 1991 when my adopted son, who I had never, ever forgotten or stopped loving, turned 18 years of age. I knew he was legally an adult now so I could apply for identifying information about him if he or his parents hadn't put a block on his information being released. I talked with Gary who was very uncomfortable talking about my adopted son. I always thought he was concerned that our family might be upset or disrupted in some way if my adopted son came back into my life. I said I wanted to apply for identifying information about my adopted son and I was going to do it. He probably felt uneasy about this but he did not try to dissuade me from doing so. I had had many years of self-therapy as I completed my studies so I felt ready to find out more about my son now. I applied for the information from the department and paid the fee involved and waited for a response. Before too long I received a large envelope, which contained information and a copy of the original birth certificate which had my name on it as his biological mother and the details of my son. He had been named Alan. It was a lot to take in for me and I was 33 by this time. I wondered if 18 years was too young for him to handle me coming into his life at this time. I also wondered what he thought of me and whether he would even want to meet me at all. I imagined he would be very angry at me and I had no idea what his adoptive parents would think of me trying to make contact with him. It was a little scary for me to do as well. So, I decided 18 was too young for him to deal with all of this and I would wait until he was much older before making contact with him.

It was during this time, in Townsville, I decided to tell our three children about their adopted older brother. I spoke to them all individually, on our own, as I was unsure what reactions I might get from each of them. It was such a difficult thing to do, to tell them about another sibling they had, which they'd had no idea about at all. It felt to me like they were looking at me like I had betrayed them. Each of them asked me a lot of questions and there were tears but my biggest fear was that they would think much less of me or they would feel hurt and betrayed that I hadn't told them much earlier in their lives. I tried to explain why this was not something I could have done before but I wanted them to know now that they were older. In their own way they each coped with the news and after that it was not spoken of again. For several more years, the secret was still kept secret.

During the second year of studying my social work degree at James Cook University in Townsville some of my lecturers suggested I should consider undertaking honours. I didn't know much about that, so I asked them to explain it to me, what it entailed and why they thought I should do it.

It was explained that undertaking honours would teach me research skills. I would learn how to 'do' research and analyse data and write up the findings in a rigorous, academic manner and then publish those findings. I was told having research skills is very advantageous and good skills to have. I could complete my honours either as an undergraduate or as a postgraduate but was advised, as my grades had been very good, I should think about doing honours as an undergraduate. That way, when I graduated, I would graduate with a social work degree with honours.

It all sounded very hard to me and I wasn't sure I could do it. I spoke to several of the lecturers and to other students who were also contemplating doing honours. I spoke to Professor Ros Thorpe, at the university whom I greatly admired, respected and trusted her opinion. She had been very encouraging of me doing honours and reassured me that I could do it. So even though I wasn't sure about this or believed in myself, I thought "all these other intelligent people, whose opinions I respect, seem to think I can do this", so based on their belief in me, I decided to take another leap of faith and give it a go, even though I still doubted myself.

I enrolled in honours as an undergraduate and it felt like I had taken a step out into a black abyss and I just hoped I would be able to work out how to 'do' this research honours thing. I chose the topic of exploring the life experiences of women living in a coal mining town, from a socialist feminist perspective. I went back out to the mining areas south west of Mackay to interview research participants as part of this research. My supervisor was Professor Thorpe who had always been so encouraging of me throughout the years of my study with James Cook University and with her guidance, expertise and belief in me, I navigated the various stages of entering a research project through to completion two years later. It took me two years rather than one as I had started another, full-time job, as the coordinator of a youth crime prevention program in Thuringowa. That was a whole other year of working with young people engaged in the youth justice system, or those who were on the fringe of the youth justice system, and my job (and the youth workers I managed) was to try and keep them out of the youth justice system. What a challenge that was, but it was a lot of fun as we came up with all sorts of creative ideas to positively engage young people and keep them out of trouble with the law.

Amazingly, at the end of my second year of my research honours, I graduated with a Bachelor of Social Work Degree with First Class Honours. I published a journal article from this research and was subsequently contacted by *Marie Claire* magazine who asked if I would be interviewed about the research I had completed. I was very honoured but unfortunately I had to decline, as I had promised the research participants I would not divulge the name of the mining town where I had undertaken the research and *Marie Claire* wanted the town named, so I was in a bind, but I had given my word, so I couldn't be a part of the magazine article, which was a shame but I was committed to honouring my word to the women who had entrusted me with their stories for the research.

I was offered casual work as a tutor within the School of Social Work and as a research assistant at James Cook University. I eagerly accepted these casual positions as I was not ready to leave the university altogether, but my course was finished. I was keen to assist with other research and keep connected to the university and the people there who I had come to know and consider my colleagues and friends. I worked with other research assistants and principal researchers to undertake research into the styles of Aboriginal and Torres Strait Islander helpers, whether they had formal training qualifications or whether they were seen as cultural Elders and helpers within their respective communities.

It was such a privileged position for me to be in as it gave me a depth of insight into the differing cultural groups and the intracultural groups as well. A monograph was published as a result of the research titled *Murri Way* which I believe is still referred to in some universities today.

World of Possibilities

I am so glad I held my breath, took a risk and jumped off the edge of that cliff into what felt like a big, unknown and scary black abyss, called honours. As it turned out, it was a very worthwhile risk to take, in the long run.

CHAPTER 8

FINAL PIECES OF THE PUZZLE

At the end of 1994, when I'd finished my Social Work Honours degree, Gary and I and our children had been living in Townsville for four years. Gary and the boys were very involved in junior rugby league football, Gary as a junior coach and the boys both played football as well. Heather was playing netball too, so we were all very heavily involved in the Townsville community where the children had made friends, as had we. We were trying to decide whether to settle down roots and stay in Townsville permanently or whether to return to our hometown of Mackay. We vacillated between staying and leaving so many times. We'd go house hunting in Townsville when we thought we were going to stay because we wanted to upgrade our house but then we weren't sure if we should return to Mackay where my mother and Gary's parents all lived, and where we had numerous extended family members, particularly on Gary's side of the family. We thought it would be good for the children to get to know all of their relatives and we also thought there might be more opportunities for the kids back in Mackay where we still knew so many people from our school days or through sport or through our extended family there.

In the end, a state government job was advertised for a Youth Development Officer with the Department of Tourism, Sport and Youth in Mackay and as I'd had experience working with youth, in both the shelter and the youth justice program, and I'd worked as a community development worker in Dysart, I thought I would apply. Gary and I agreed, if I got the job then that would make our decision for us: we would return to live in Mackay. So that's what I did. I applied for the job, went for the interview and got the job, and we relocated from Townsville back to Mackay over the Christmas holiday break so I was ready to start the new position in Mackay and the kids could be settled into new schools for the commencement of 1995.

The next part of the adventure was underway for our family and it was exciting to be coming home after living away for 13 years in Dysart and then Townsville.

We put our green garden waste business on the market, not even sure if it would sell or whether we would have to walk away from it, but in the end it did sell and we didn't lose on the sale, which was a miracle, we both thought. It was a good outcome in the end. We also put our house in Townsville on the market and moved back to Mackay while we waited for it to sell. We needed it to sell before we could buy another house in Mackay; in the meantime, we split ourselves and lived with our families. Eventually, the Townsville house sold, although we had to drop the price significantly to sell, but at least all of our ties to Townsville had been settled and we could buy our own home in Mackay and all be back living together again.

We looked around Mackay and found our new home in South Mackay which was close to both of our parents' homes. It was a

Final Pieces of the Puzzle

large, lowset, brick family home with a lovely entertaining area at the back and a large inground pool which we all loved. It was a great family home in which to bring up our kids and for them to have their friends visit and have sleepovers and pool parties. It was the perfect house for our family and we did a lot of internal renovations to modernise it during the 19 years that we lived there.

I settled into my new job with the department and began to meet many others in the social welfare field in Mackay and the region. I enjoyed my job very much and I enjoyed being back working for government again. It gave me a sense of job security with good pay and conditions so I felt very fortunate to have the position I was in.

Many of the youth services which still exist in Mackay and the region today came into being during the time I was working in the youth development officer's role. It was a time of great collaboration with other services and individuals and as a result several applications for funding to start up new services were successful during that time. Many are still operating in Mackay to this day, i.e. the Youth Information and Referral Service (YIRS) and the Youth Worker position in Sarina are just a couple of examples. I was 37 by this time and felt truly lucky in work and life. Things were good for our family, just the usual family ups and downs, and I felt very fortunate to be in the position I was in.

Gary got a job with a local engineering firm doing trades assistant work and after work and on weekends he was back coaching junior rugby league. The boys also played footy again and Heather got into sport and a modelling school where she learned about personal grooming and deportment. She loved it.

It wasn't long before Gary was offered a job as a part-time junior development coach which he keenly accepted, taking on this second job, which was not a chore as he loved the game and he relished in the company of other men and boys, and the whole football culture.

Although I was working full time in my departmental job, I still found that I was looking for something more to do for myself. After all, I had been working and studying and raising children in Townsville and it seemed to me that I wasn't doing enough with my time. I did of course go and watch the kids play in their various sporting events but I felt the need to do something more, for myself.

I started looking around and I saw an advertisement for a casual TAFE teacher's position in the Community Services Diploma course they offered and I applied for the position and ended up getting the job. I thoroughly enjoyed being back in a casual teaching role, as I had tutored students at James Cook University in Townsville, so it was a familiar and comfortable environment for me. I taught classes in two subjects for one year which meant I was teaching two evenings each week to students who were looking to start a career in the community services industry. I met some wonderful people who had amazing life experiences and, as adults, they were keen to seek a new direction in their work or in their life. They were so enthusiastic and keen to learn, they were like sponges. Such a pleasure to teach. Many of these students went on to undertake higher study and complete degrees at university level and have since gained very good positions in the community.

Towards the end of that first year of teaching at TAFE I was approached by Gordon, the man who had started me on the path to my own study 14 years earlier in Dysart; he was still working for TAFE. Gordon was also the Mackay representative of James Cook University and he asked if I would be interested in teaching students at the small study centre operated by James Cook University in Mackay. I was asked to tutor in the degree programs of Social Work and Community Welfare and Professor Thorpe, who had mentored me in Townsville and supervised my honours research, had oversight of the implementation of these new flexible learning courses to be offered in Mackay. Of course, I said yes, and at the commencement of the next academic year, I started tutoring students for one or two evenings each week, after my day job. I really enjoyed assisting students to grasp and understand the concepts they were learning in their courses and clearly seeing when the 'light bulbs' went off in their heads and I knew they 'got it'. They understood the information they were learning about from their study materials. That is such a rewarding experience as a teacher. The down side was there was always assignment marking on the weekends, which I didn't mind initially but as the years of teaching went by this became more of a chore.

As a teacher, I must admit I did feel I was somewhat of a fraud. I mean, who was I to be teaching anyone? I didn't even have a teaching qualification and I wondered if I had done any teacher training what more could I be providing to students? Perhaps there was a lot more I could be doing to assist their learning experience which I wasn't even aware of, given I'd never completed any teacher training. This set me on a path to explore what courses were available for me to learn about teaching and gain a teaching qualification. Eventually, I found a course which was a Post Graduate Diploma of Arts (Adult Education and Training). So, once again, I immersed myself in study and relished everything I was learning. It took me two years of part-time study to complete this course and I thoroughly enjoyed it. Apart from the teaching and evaluation subjects, there were two electives offered and I could choose any subjects I wanted to study from any of the other humanities faculties.

This was exciting; I knew I had a deficit in my knowledge of history and there was a contemporary history subject offered which I enrolled in and learnt so much about world history from the 1500s. It was so interesting, and I learned many amazing events from modern history, which I thoroughly enjoyed. The other elective I took up was a subject called 'Teaching Thinking'. How wonderful to have the opportunity to learn about how to teach others to think creatively and critically. Again, this was another subject which greatly enhanced my own learning, knowledge and thinking on how to teach students.

I worked as a casual tutor for James Cook University for 16 years in total, so I saw many students enter the courses and graduate in this time, many of whom I am still friends with or have worked with or supervised since that time. I was very fortunate to also work with other tutors who were leaders in the community and I made many good friends during these years. Overall, it was a very rewarding role, albeit in addition to my full-time job within government, throughout the duration of my time as a casual teacher.

As governments come and go with each election cycle, so did the machinery of government changes occur with regularity each three years in Queensland and sometimes within the three-year cycle of government elections. As a result, the position I held within the Department of Tourism, Sport and Youth was transitioned to the Department of Family and Community Services after the Goss Labor Government lost the 1996 election to the conservative parties and Rob Borbidge became Queensland Premier.

The department my position went to was very resource poor compared to the department I'd come from, and the senior supervisors were quick to strip my role of some of the meagre benefits (such as a vehicle, administration support and petty cash) which came with me into the new department. I found it a little unsettling for quite a while and this set me on a path of looking around for any other opportunities that may have been available.

In another area of this new department there was the Youth Justice service. This interested me as it was an area of work with which I was familiar from my earlier days of working in the youth programs in Townsville. An opportunity came up to move into that service area so I applied and was very fortunate to be able to move into that role which I enjoyed and fulfilled for the next two years.

The Youth Justice service was located within the same office as the child protection services, which was an area I had never held any desire to work within. The same manager managed both youth justice and child protection within the office, so these staff were my office colleagues. I worked alongside the child protection workers in the same office and we shared the same lunch room, so it was inevitable that I became interested in and drawn into their discussions and the world of child protection practice opened up to me.

An opportunity became available as the Youth Justice Team Leader, which was a higher-level position than I was in, and the pay was better too. I decided to try for that position so submitted my application and was fortunate enough to get the job and move into the role. Once in a Team Leader role there were times when I needed to assist other Team Leaders working in child protection so the lines between youth justice and child protection became very blurred and I eventually moved out of youth justice completely and into the Team Leader's position working with children and families.

It was such a complex and contested field of practice where I committed myself to for the next 14 years and gave it my all.

CHAPTER 9

MY YEARS AS AN OCTOPUS

By now it's the mid-1990s and life is hectic. The kids are teenagers, either in high school or working, and still pursuing all of their extracurricular and social activities, as they had always done. Gary was still working hard. He had started another green waste collection business in Mackay, in addition to the full-time football manager's job he held with Souths Rugby League Club. Every year, for many years, Gary recruited footballers from out of town to the club and until they could find a place of their own, we always had another footballer or two who lived with us each year. This usually ended up with them staying with us for the duration of the footy season, which turned out okay because many have remained good friends who we still keep in contact with from those days.

There were all of the kids' friends coming and going from our place and all of the usual activities that teenagers 'need' to be involved in. A neighbour once asked me what we did at our house because there were always so many cars at our place with young people coming and going. I think she thought we were selling drugs or something but we were just a very busy family with lots of our kids' friends, and our friends, coming and going for different reasons, for barbeques and other social activities a lot of the time. Life was very full and there was never a spare moment.

During these years I had also taken up studying again. I was keen to progress my career in the public service so I enrolled in, and completed, a Masters in Social Policy which took me four years part time. I was still tutoring in the evenings and working full time. I was also managing to fit in visits with my mother and other family members on weekends, and keeping up with the usual school events that parents need to attend, while also attending social gatherings with the kids, our friends or with work colleagues.

Life was full; it was a real balancing act during those years. I don't think I have ever worked so hard in my life between home, family, study and work. Working in the Department of Child Safety was also the busiest time of my working life. It was hectic working there with huge caseloads and staff to supervise and never being able to please everyone; no matter what decision was made, it was always the wrong decision, from someone's perspective. It was also the best place to work as I worked with some amazing people who went over and beyond to do their best to ensure the safety of the children they worked with, but this never gets reported in the media. We all worked hard and for long hours each day there. Sometimes I might want to go to the toilet in the morning but wouldn't get there until late afternoon, it was that busy. Many of the staff I worked with during these years are still close friends and colleagues of mine.

Eventually, I moved from the Team Leader's role into a Senior Practitioner's position which I enjoyed. I could focus on child protection practice while not also having to be so involved in staff supervision and management. This was a welcome change, as managing some staff could be time consuming and very challenging at times.

When Anna Bligh was premier in 2000, she introduced a doctoral research scholarship program within the Department of Child Safety. It was meant to be offered every year but, as it turned out, it was offered only once, much to the chagrin of many departmental staff who told me they'd intended to apply in subsequent years, so they didn't get the opportunity to do that.

There were three scholarships offered, two in southern Queensland and one in the north. It was offered for all departmental staff to apply for and, as I had been thinking of an area within the child protection field, which I believed could benefit from more research, I decided to apply for a departmental scholarship. If successful, it meant I could undertake full-time research, on my nominated topic, as my full-time paying job, for the next three years. It was too good an opportunity to not go for. So, I threw my hat in the ring, completed the application forms, went for an interview at James Cook University, where I would be again studying, if successful, then I waited to hear the outcome. You can imagine my delight when I was informed that my application had been successful and the topic of researching 'the education, training and support needs of foster carers' was given the nod of approval to proceed. I was thrilled and my family were thrilled for me too!

So, in 2001, I embarked on undertaking a research doctorate, as an employee of the department. I arranged to work from the Mackay Study Centre of James Cook University, which meant I had an office base to work from, and could maintain a routine of going to and from work which meant I had the separation between home and work which I needed to focus on the research ahead of me. If I was trying to work from home, I knew I would have a lot of family and friends dropping by to say hello or stop in for a cuppa and a chat. I knew that many of them didn't fully understand what it was I was 'really' doing, which is perfectly understandable as not too many people, particularly mums in the suburbs, decide to undertake doctoral research. So, I understood and knew I needed to have a separate workplace for this research to be completed if I was going to do the job well. I was bonded to the department for three years after completing the research which meant I had to stay working for them for that period of time after completing the doctorate. However, that was not a concern to me; I had no plans to leave the department and I genuinely hoped the research I was to undertake was going to be beneficial to the department, to foster carers, and most importantly, to the children fostered into their care.

I had seen too many well-intentioned foster carers unintentionally cause further harm to children in their care because they were largely unaware of the impact of trauma on children from prolonged abuse or neglect which they had experienced. There were some exceptionally good foster carers but there were fewer of them than was needed. Therefore, it was my view that the majority of foster carers were ill-equipped to know how best to respond to and care for those traumatised children who have myriad complex and sensitive issues to respond to. I had hoped with the best evidence-based training available, foster carers would be better trained, informed and supported and therefore, be better able to respond to the care needs of these vulnerable children and adolescents in their care, all of whom had been abused and/or neglected and traumatised to varying degrees during their young lives.

It was my good fortune that Professor Ros Thorpe who had supervised my honours research also agreed to supervise my doctoral research. She is one person who has had such a hugely positive influence on my life and I have come to realise that none of us can achieve to our fullest potential without having such supportive, nurturing, encouraging, patient mentors as what she was to me. I am truly grateful to her for her belief in me which, undoubtedly, spurred me on to keep aiming for higher goals to achieve, until I did eventually reach the highest academic goal of completing my PhD at the end of 2004.

I have come to understand and accept that each one of us who is supported by others to achieve beyond our wildest dreams has a responsibility to 'pay it forward'. I know I certainly have that strong sense of responsibility to others and as such I have sought out opportunities to support and mentor others both through formal mentoring programs, within the department, and outside of that, for young people who have needed some direction and support which I have been willing and able to provide. Seeing these people succeed brings with it such a strong sense of satisfaction and accomplishment that I have been able to assist someone else on their life's journey, just as I have been fortunate to have others support and mentor me during mine. I do believe this is the essence of our being.

During the years of completing my PhD there were several significant personal and family events which occurred that meant I needed to be more available to family than focusing on my research at the time.

In 2001 my mother suffered a minor stroke which left her with an inability to do the things she had always done previously, such as cooking and gardening and general household activities, which she took great pleasure from. My siblings and I all rallied to support her through this time. I needed time away from my research to spend with her and support her as best I could.

During these busiest years of my life, prior to my mother having a stroke, the pain in my hip, and deferred pain emanating from it down my right leg to my knee, had become almost unbearable again. I could feel my hip joint 'slip' unexpectedly, and I never knew if my hip was going to stay firm or slip, which gave me a sudden jolt when it happened and I thought I would fall over each time. Whenever I went to a shopping centre, I would always hold on to a shopping trolly, whether I needed one or not. It provided me with a sense of security and safety, should my hip suddenly 'give way' on me. I could only walk very slowly for this reason too. The deterioration of my hip was really starting to slow my mobility down again and this was annoying as I had so much I needed to be doing.

The doctors told me I needed a second hip replacement, or a 'revision', as they called it. I couldn't do this just now, as I felt my mother needed me, and I was also very scared of going through such a big operation again, especially when I got so sick after the last one, although that was 20 years ago now.

I managed to put it off for another year or so but in 2002 I had no choice, I had to get it done again, and the hip replacement operation was booked in for February that year. Fortunately for me it was a much better experience this time round. No pain at all due to the wonderful pain management plan they had put in place for me and my rehabilitation went very smoothly as well. Gary was such a huge help at home after the operation which also made things so much easier for me. I was pleased it was over and done with, so I could get on with my life and finishing my PhD, or so I thought.

Later that same year, as I returned to refocus on my doctoral research work again, I sat down at my computer and checked my emails. There were the usual generic emails sent around by the university to all staff and then there seemed to be some spam emails which I was deleting, and I almost deleted an email from someone whose name I didn't recognise, but for some reason, which I am eternally grateful for, I didn't. Instead, I opened it, and began to read. It started out something along the lines of "… I am sorry to bother you and I don't mean to cause you any distress but I am trying to make contact with my mother and I think that could be you …"

That email went on with more words but I cannot remember anything after reading that line. I literally just about fell off my chair. I was so nervous, excited, yet scared, and I had no one to talk to, or jump up and down with, and say, "Guess what's just happened?" I was feeling anxious and I needed to speak to someone, so I phoned my daughter, Heather, and told her. She was just as excited as me and I read the email out to her in full. She asked me what I was going to do and I said, "I'm going to respond to him and see where it goes." Which is exactly what I did.

I emailed him back and asked him about his date and place of birth and how old he was and our emails went back and forth and we both became very excited as we realised and accepted that we had finally connected with each other, mother and son. It was a very emotional time for us both.

We exchanged some photos online over the following weeks and it was agreed we would arrange to meet each other in Brisbane, which we did in August of 2003. Heather came with me. It was so exciting to be able to see him and hug him and hold him. He came with photo albums of his childhood for me to see. It was lovely. I talked to him about the circumstances of his adoption and asked if he was angry at me. He said he wasn't, that he'd had a good life. We talked and talked for at least a couple of hours, then we walked back to where Heather and his fiancé had been waiting for us at a nearby cafe. He later told me it was at the constant urging of his fiancé and her mother that prompted him to take the scary step of reaching out to me. I talked to him about my earlier attempt to make contact with him and asked if he knew about that, as I'd always wondered if he was really told that I'd tried to make contact with him. It was a few years earlier, when he was 25 years old.

After receiving his identifying information in 1991, I had waited from when he was 18 until he was 25 before attempting to contact him.

In hindsight, I should have used an intermediary, but I didn't and I cold called his adoptive mother and explained who I was and why I was calling. It was not the best way to handle this and consequently, I was not well received, to say the least, and the conversation soon ended. Not long after that call, the next day, her husband phoned me back and advised he would talk to his son and explain that I had made contact, for which I was grateful. A few days later he recontacted me and said he had spoken to his son who wanted nothing to do with me and I was not to recontact and upset his wife again, which I again apologised for doing. I asked only one thing of him at the end of that phone call and that was that my name and contact details be given to their son, so if he ever changed his mind, he would know my name and how to make contact with me. He said he would do that for me but I always wondered if any of this really happened at all, whether he would, in fact, pass on my contact details to his son.

Now, four years later, I asked my son, Alan, if any of this had actually occurred. He said he was told, but out of respect for his mother, who reared him, he didn't feel he could make contact with me, which I understood and accepted. He and I have remained in contact with each other ever since this time in 2002.

His adoptive mother had since sadly passed away, but it enabled me, along with Gary, to attend Alan's second wedding, which was wonderful to be a part of. He is now happily married to a lovely woman, Kate, and they have two beautiful boys, my grandsons, who I am able to watch grow up and be a part of their lives. We have come full circle, and it is wonderful, and so satisfying. Now on his birthday each year, I can celebrate it with him, whereas before we reconnected it was always such a sad time for me—before, during and after his birthday. He calls me on Mother's Day each year and we always comment about how nice it is to be able to share in these special occasions with each other now.

"Alan and Kate's Wedding with Gary and me"

What a huge year 2002 had been for me and my family! So much high emotion to deal with and work through but now, again, it was time to refocus on the doctoral research which I did until the next unexpected tragedy occurred in my family.

It was 2003 and our son, Ross, was involved in an horrific highspeed car accident and he broke his neck. He had to be airlifted to the Mackay Base Hospital. It was so distressing to see your own child, even though he was an adult of 23 years by now, go through that, not knowing if he would live or die, while we waited for the chopper to land at the hospital. We saw him briefly before he was rushed into emergency surgery. We were told he had head injuries and a fractured vertebra. Waiting was agonising while he was in surgery, not knowing whether he'd have brain damage or whether he'd be able to walk again or not.

My imagination ran wild. I couldn't help it. I was so worried about him.

After surgery we were told he'd fractured his C3 vertebrae but it was just holding on by a small thread of bone, so he was being fitted with a halo brace to enable the vertebrae to mend and, all going well, he would not lose the use of his arms or legs. It was so hard to see him in that halo brace for the next six months, every few weeks getting the screws into his head tightened, which was so painful for him. Thankfully, however, he would recover and not become a paraplegic or quadriplegic, which he'd been so close to becoming. It was such a stressful time for our family but thankfully, over time, he eventually made a full recovery.

Around the same time as Ross had his accident Gary's mother was diagnosed with a brain tumour. It was devastating for her and Gary's dad and for us all. I knew how worried she was feeling so I tried to focus on the positive aspects of there being treatment available and the planned surgery would remove the tumour and she would soon recover. I'm not sure she was convinced about that but, nevertheless, just being together with her, my father-in-law and Gary seemed to bring her a little hope, and some comfort and relief, enough to be able to cope with each day, at least.

Gary is an only child so the four of us and our children are her immediate family. She was flown to Townsville soon after her diagnosis, where she underwent neurosurgery to remove the tumour, but it was quite advanced and had multiple tentacles extending within her brain, we were told, so they were unable to remove it all. Eventually it took hold again. It was an aggressive form of brain cancer.

She stayed in Townsville hospital for a couple of months before being transferred back to Mackay hospital for another few months but she never came out of hospital and passed away in July 2003. It had been seven months from diagnosis to her passing and Gary and I did all we could during that time to be with her and also support Gary's dad. It was important for us to be there for them both during these months, and then through the following months and years of being there for Gary's dad as well.

The years from 2001 to 2003 had been very difficult years for our family and I tried my best to be available and support everyone as best I could during these years. Now it was time to return to completing my PhD. I focused my energy on my research, still diligently treating it like my job, every day. My supervisor was wonderful during these years and very understanding of the reasons why my research was not on track as it should have been. Nevertheless, I put my head down and worked as hard as I could to complete my doctoral thesis by the end of 2004, which, thankfully, I finally did. What a huge sense of relief when I submitted my thesis. It was done! Such a wonderful sense of accomplishment. It was my Mount Everest and I had climbed it and planted the flag on top. I'd done it for myself and was proud I'd stuck with it throughout so many significant family events which occurred during my research.

Gary came to my graduation where I was awarded the Doctorate of Philosophy in the Discipline of Social Work. He congratulated me as Doctor Butcher for the first time. It was so strange to hear myself be referred to as 'Doctor'. He told me how proud he was of me and he said, "You should write a book about your life one day." I laughed at him, thinking there is no way I would ever write a book about my life. I mean, who would ever be interested in my life?

I Ruined My Life ... Or So They Said

"My PhD Graduation from James Cook University"

I returned to work at the department in the Senior Practitioner role but soon after returning to work, the manager's position at Child Safety became available. The Regional Director in the department encouraged me to apply for the position, which I did, and fortunately I was successful and took up that position in 2006. I held it for the next five years, until I really could not do that very challenging and complex work any longer. I knew it was time for a change. By now it had been 16 years of working in the department in various roles and I had seen and heard so many distressing situations for children and adolescents that I realised

I just couldn't do it anymore. The time had come for me to have a long break, if not resign altogether.

I spoke to my supervisor and let her know how I was feeling and I asked for 12 months leave, on half pay, as I had a lot of recreation leave and long service leave owing to me. If she had not approved this leave I intended on resigning, but to my surprise, she did approve my leave request and I felt a sense of relief, as I knew I could have a long break after working all my life from the age of 15 to 53, which I now was. I had worked hard, studied, tutored, been a wife, mother and daughter for many years, and now I could have a well-earned break to catch my breath, before I started again.

CHAPTER 10

THE UNEXPECTED BLESSING

It was 2011 and this was my year. A year of doing what I wanted to do. The kids were all grown up by this time—Ross was 31, Brad, 28, and Heather, 25—so they were all off doing their own thing and there was just Gary and me at home again. Although by this time Gary was as busy as ever. He was no longer involved in football in any capacity. He'd changed jobs and moved into management positions and he was at this time working as a manager and partner in another business.

I had more time to spend with my mother and I made sure I visited her every day. We would usually have morning tea together, or I would take her shopping, or just spend time with her. Sometimes my sister would join us and we had a couple of very memorable shopping escapades. My mother was not very mobile, so when we took her shopping, we usually got a wheelchair for her to make it easier and faster to get around the shopping centre. I remember one particular time when my sister and I took Mum for lunch and then we hit the dress shops together, the three of us. We had a lovely afternoon with lots of laughter along the way. We kept finding clothes we thought Mum would like, and she did. So, she started to pile them up on her lap. When we got to the checkout, she had a pile of clothes on her lap which she could hardly see over. There were sales on, so it didn't really cost that much and I didn't care if she never wore them because I just delighted in seeing her have fun and be happy buying them with us. We had lots of laughs with Mum that day and it is a lovely memory I will keep always, of the three of us together.

During my 'gap year' away from work I decided there were some things I really wanted to do for myself. I wanted to learn Tai Chi, so I enrolled in weekly lessons which I attended and thoroughly enjoyed throughout the year. The second thing I wanted to do was to learn Italian, as I'd learnt Italian at high school and one of my best friends was Italian so we used to speak it together at school and at her home on weekends, back in our school days. I wanted to pick that up again, so I did. I enrolled in the language college in our town and attended night classes to learn Italian lessons for most of that year. I really enjoyed learning Italian and I would love to live in Italy to fully immerse myself in the language and the culture. To be good at it you have to be forced to speak it every day and I would so love to do that if I could. I have visited Italy with Gary and I did speak a little Italian there. I was delighted when I was actually understood as I ordered coffee and cake for us in a café in Venice.

The third thing I wanted to do during the 'gap year' was to take up genealogy and research my family trees. I became fully engaged in this activity and learned so much about my family history on both my mothers and father's sides of the family. This was very interesting and I became fully engrossed in what I was unearthing of our family history. I would often talk for hours with my mother about what I was finding out, particularly about her side of the

The Unexpected Blessing

family. She often had more information to add or suggested I speak to one of her siblings to get more details, which I did, and I recorded all of this information in the family tree. We had some really interesting conversations about our ancestry and there were many new pieces of information which I provided to Mum about her side of the family and also about my father's side of the family, which she found very interesting. Particularly information about her father's war service during WW1. I sent away and got his war records and we pored over them together as she recounted tales her father had told her as a child about his service in the war on the western front of Belgium and France.

This time spent with Mum in 2011 was very much a blessing for me and if I had not taken that time off work it would not have happened. How fortunate was I that it worked out this way?

I would call in to her house and see her after Tai Chi or after attending my Italian lessons and we would always have a cuppa and a talk. I think she enjoyed the company as much as I did. It was a lovely time spent with her. I think she sometimes wondered where I'd come from, as my interests were so different to anyone else's in my family. She would smile and say, "You're always doing something different, Anne", but I think she was proud of the fact that I was always doing something I enjoyed.

Quite unexpectedly during 2011 my mother, whose health had been failing for the past few years and she'd lost a lot of weight, had a very bad fall in the kitchen at her house where she still lived with my younger brother, although he was not at home at the time of the fall.

My mother was wearing a medic alert alarm which she later told us she had pressed and pressed many times while lying on the kitchen floor. She could not get up and I think she knew her leg was broken. It was a compound fracture and her leg was positioned awkwardly in an unnatural position. My older brother was called by the security firm monitoring the medic alert. He was the first to arrive at the house where he found her on the floor in the kitchen. He tried to help her as best he could but there was little he could do until the ambulance arrived, which thankfully they soon did. They administered pain relief for her and somehow managed to get her onto a stretcher and take her to the hospital where she required immediate surgery to insert a plate and screws to hold her hip joint in place.

Along with other family members I went to the hospital to wait and see how she was going to be. She came out of surgery and was returned to a private room where she had to wear a pressure pump that inflated and deflated every few minutes to keep the blood circulation flowing in her leg. It was cruel to watch her flinch in pain every time the pressure pump inflated as it was obviously placing some movement in the hip joint that had just been operated on. I asked many times for the nursing staff to give her more pain relief which they did until they could give her no more. I stayed with her that whole night as I sensed she was scared and I didn't want to leave her alone, so I held her hand and sat with her.

She was starting to experience other complications due to the anaesthesia and pain relief she'd had as her kidneys had not been functioning all that well before the fall. After all of the anaesthesia and pain relief drugs, the kidney functioning had reduced to dangerous levels. She had to be transferred to the public hospital where she had to be placed on to kidney dialysis. This happened quickly and she was sedated in ICU for the next few days. She drifted in and out of consciousness during these days but could talk to us at times and she knew we were there with her. Eventually her other organs started shutting down and the hospital staff talked to my siblings and I and asked us what we wanted to do and whether we knew what our mother's wishes were. We all agreed she had been through enough and we didn't want to put her through any more pain or discomfort, so the nursing staff removed all of the tubes and we stayed with her until the end. All four of us, her children, were with her, telling her how much we loved her and thanking her for being such a wonderful mother to us all. She knew she was going. She said to me, the one who she'd always said was a 'strong girl', that she thought this was it. I told her she was strong and if anyone could come through this, she could. I knew she wouldn't, I just wanted to give her some hope. She was 80 years of age.

She had been a wonderful, selfless mother to us all. She'd worked hard her entire life and we were blessed to be able to call her our mother.

"Mum and me"

CHAPTER 11

MY BLESSED LIFE TODAY

The end of my 'gap year' was drawing to a close and I was thinking I would have to return to the Department of Child Safety. I had realised in my year away from this field of practice that my heart was no longer in it and I really felt I needed to do something else, something new, something different, something energising and interesting.

As luck would have it, at around the same time I became aware of a new manager's position being created in the Department of Communities, Child Safety and Disability Services in Mackay. The position was at the same level as my position in Child Safety, so if I applied and got it, it would be a sideways move for me, but I would be no worse off at all. This position was the same level, at the same pay rate, with the same employment conditions.

Even though I had studied a disability elective subject at university, I wasn't sure about working in Disability Services. I'd never thought of it as an area of practice for me but I knew I needed a change, so

I applied for the manager's position in Disability Services and went for an interview for the position. Not too long afterwards, I was contacted and advised I had been successful and I was offered the position. I was so excited again. I couldn't get over how fortunate I was to be able to continue working as a manager in government in this newly created position in Mackay.

I started in the role in August 2011 and as I became familiar with the world of disability services, I was so amazed at what I was seeing. All of these wonderful families who were so committed to their sons or daughters or other family members with disabilities, many of whom had cared for them all of their lives, so selflessly and so lovingly. There were elderly parents in their 90s still caring for adult children in their 60s and 70s with disabilities. It was truly awe-inspiring and I noticed it so acutely, I think, because I had worked in Child Safety for so many years where I saw many parents who put their own needs ahead of their children's needs, whether that was as a result of a drug addiction, or mental health problems, or poverty, or simply because of self-indulgence, and placing their relationships with their partner over and above the needs of their children. I had seen it all and now I was seeing the exact flip side of those scenarios where there were parents who went over and beyond what they needed to do or could, in fact, manage, without any thought that the government should step in and help them in their roles. They had no expectations, or sense of entitlement, of receiving any government support whatsoever. And, anything they did get, they were extremely grateful for. It was amazing to me and such a stark contrast to what I'd seen in Child Safety, where I had worked for the best part of the last two decades.

I very much enjoyed my time at Disability Services where I learnt so much about people with disabilities, about their carers, family members, and the entire disability service system in Queensland. All of those involved in this sphere of work were quite inspirational to me. I worked in the manager's role there for another five years and had several long stints acting as North Queensland Regional Director during this time, when my boss was away doing other work. I could easily have stayed in the manager's role that I loved so much until I retired. I enjoyed working with colleagues there for whom I have the utmost respect and regard; however, a little thing called the National Disability Insurance Scheme (NDIS) came along and the Queensland Government committed to phase out of being a provider of disability services. The government then set about transitioning all of the Queensland disability services staff out of their jobs over the next three years. As the manager of my service centre, it was my role to lead the transition out of disability services for my office and my staff, and for myself.

I had to lead myself out of a job and do it while encouraging others that there would be a world of employment opportunities coming along which they could avail themselves of. I did believe there would be numerous opportunities for staff, either within other government departments or within the community sector, and all staff either found jobs in other departments or the non-government sector or they accepted a voluntary redundancy package.

I had hoped our region of North Queensland would be one of the last to transition to the NDIS which would give me another three years in my position in the department, but instead, we were the first region to begin the transition. This led me to start looking around for what else I might do, as I was not ready yet for retirement. The department was very clear there would be no forced redundancies of any staff, which was good because it meant I still had tenure with the department.

I decided to apply for 12 months' leave from the department when another friend and colleague suggested I apply for a position as a Senior Research Fellow at the Queensland Centre for Domestic and

Family Violence Research, which is situated within the Mackay Campus of Central Queensland University. Domestic violence was not a specific field I had practised in before but every job I'd ever had consisted of working with people who had experienced or were experiencing domestic and family violence. Of course, I also had a very personal experience of that in my younger life, not that that made me eligible to apply for this position. It was my research background that provided me with the advantage of applying for this position and the fact I had completed a doctorate. In universities it is very important to have staff employed in either teaching or research who have completed a PhD so having that behind me was essential for the position I was applying for.

I was offered a 12-month contract in that position, which suited me perfectly. It lined up with the length of time I had applied for leave from the department and, as I wasn't sure if I wanted to be a full-time researcher, or even know if I would like working as a researcher in academia, I accepted the offer and began working at the university. I learned so much about this specific field of practice in that year. It was such a wonderful opportunity to have a year of reading and researching in this field and totally immersing myself in the theory, practice, research and evidence base of this field which I remain so grateful for the opportunity to have gained this experience. The knowledge which I attained in that year has certainly greatly assisted me to transition into the next new position in my career.

In realising that research was not so enthralling or exciting as being in a management or practice role, I was wondering what I might do next when my 12-month contract was up. I knew I could go back to the department and they would find a job for me, and I was eventually offered two more manager jobs within government in Mackay, both of which I declined, because I had been approached and made another offer of employment which I was considering.

It was after a conference, hosted by the research centre at which I was working at Central Queensland University, that I was approached by two women who were members of a management committee of the local domestic and family violence service in Mackay. They had been speaking to a colleague of mine who had told them my tenure was coming to an end at the research centre but mentioned the years of management experience I had gained whilst working in government. I'm not sure what else she may have said but they approached me and asked me what I was planning on doing when my contract with the university expired. I said I wasn't exactly sure, so they asked me if I would be interested in hearing a proposal from them and of course I was curious, so I said "yes". They mentioned there was a manager's position at the community service for which they were on the management committee and asked if I would be interested in this position at all. I said I would certainly be interested in finding out more about the position, so we set a date and time for another meeting a few days later.

I attended the meeting and listened to what they were looking for in a manager for the position and I spoke about my experience in management positions in government. It seemed this experience was what they were looking for, and what I could offer was a good match, so we discussed salaries and starting dates as the position was currently vacant.

I realised I'd just been interviewed for the job and it was one of the most relaxed interviews I'd ever had because I didn't realise, until the end of it, that I'd been interviewed and I thought I may have the job. It was the best way to conduct a job interview for me. They did say they would need to discuss this with the rest of the management committee and get back to me. So, I knew it wasn't a done deal at that time and anything could happen but I felt very ready for this next career adventure, if it was to come my way.

Soon after that meeting I was contacted and offered the position formally and was provided with a letter of offer, which I signed and formally accepted. I took a voluntary redundancy from the department which was a huge step for me, as I was leaving government for the first time in 23 years. I was moving into the non-government sector in a new position at the local domestic violence service in Mackay. It was an exciting new direction for me to be taking and I found I was very invigorated by the prospects of this new role.

The domestic violence service is co-located with another, separate women's health service, within one building. At the time I started in my role there, the other service also had no manager in place. So the two separate committees, who had been working well together, agreed they would ask me to manage both services, which I agreed to. It just made sense to me to manage both services and all staff, instead of only one service and some of the staff. I could also see the potential benefits of such a collaboration between the two services for the broader community. It was a no brainer for me. I was used to managing large numbers of staff, not that there were that many staff there, compared to what I was used to, so it was very manageable for me to take on.

Soon after I started in the Executive Director's position the two services began to work as if they were one service, under the umbrella name of Mackay Women's Services. The breadth of work done at this service, where I still work today, includes women's and children's domestic violence counselling and men's behaviour change counselling (for men who use violence in their relationships), to court support for women attending court applying for domestic violence orders. The service also operates a domestic and family violence High Risk Team with representatives from many other government departments involved in this team. The purpose of it is to keep women and children safe and hold domestic violence perpetrators accountable for their actions within the justice system.

The service works very closely with police to follow up with women who have been victims of domestic violence. There are also parenting programs (for mums and dads) and many women's health programs offered at the centre. In the pre-Covid-19 times, the building we operate from would literally be buzzing with large numbers of groups and people coming in for counselling or other groups, services or programs. It is a source of real satisfaction for me to see the reach we have developed to support vulnerable women and children in our community.

When I started in the role there were 10 staff in total between the two services. Now there are 28 staff and a lot of new programs being offered. The level of community and industry support the service receives is amazing and truly humbling but also indicates we are doing something right, as the community reaches out to us almost every day to make donations of goods or services or even financial contributions. It never ceases to amaze me when we have women, or sometimes men, come into our centre and hand over a small or sizeable financial donation in recognition of the work we do because we assisted them or their daughter some time ago. It could even be years ago but they still want to give back to help others.

This is exactly where I am in my life now. I want to give forward to others too as I have been given so much by so many for which I am truly grateful and appreciative.

I am very fortunate to be doing the work I am doing, in a position I thoroughly enjoy, working with amazing staff who go the extra mile for clients every day. I never envisaged I would end up working in this field in the non-government sector, but here I am, and I am loving it. I am truly blessed.

CHAPTER 12

WHAT'S NEXT?

The year in which I wrote this book I turned 62 years of age. Gary and I celebrated our 43rd wedding anniversary. If we married on the rebound all those years ago, as others had said, then we've done all right for ourselves. I'm glad we didn't listen to any of those naysayers. We have travelled extensively overseas and had many exciting, adventurous and wonderful holidays together, both abroad and throughout Australia. We have shared all of the usual ups and downs of married life, as most couples do. There have been times when I have wanted to leave our marriage and I am sure there would have been times when Gary would have wanted to leave too. I'm glad neither of us did because, overall, we've had a loving, mostly contented married life, and raised our children together. I do feel I have had a very fortunate life, although as one wise person once said to me, "The harder you work the luckier you get", and I have found that to be true in my life. I have worked hard ever since the age of 15, but I haven't done it on my own. Gary and our children have been a constant source of support to me throughout our marriage, particularly as the kids have become adults.

I have met many wonderful people who have been so generous with their time and willingness to support me on my journey through sharing their knowledge, philosophies, beliefs and life insights which I have been very open to listening to and learning from. It has helped me to think about what I believe and what I don't believe, to deeply examine what I was raised to believe and accepted without questioning, compared to what I now consciously choose to accept and believe as an adult. If not for the study I have done and the connections with these wise people I would not have been confronted with these questions about what I believe and what I don't believe. I would not be where I am today or have achieved what I have so far, and for these reasons, I am eternally grateful to each and every single one of them. Who are those people in your life? Look for them or seek them out, because they are there, you just have to recognise them or find them, be open to learn, and ask them for their insights and guidance. You will be amazed at their generosity of spirit to support you.

As thinking people, I believe it is beneficial for us all to go through a deeply reflective process of self-questioning and self-examination of conscience, to determine who we really are *versus* who we really want to be. Are the two congruent already? If so, you are either very fortunate or not delving deeply enough to be brutally honest with yourself. This can be very hard to do but I can attest that those who do venture to confront their fundamental values and beliefs and make conscious decisions to accept some but perhaps reject others, can find a deep inner peace and stronger sense of self than could possibly be imagined before undertaking this process.

I am not advocating for any particular beliefs, just advocating for this as a deeply personal process for all thinking people to go through at some time in their adult lives. It helps you to find the real you, just for yourself, not for anyone else. It can bring a strong sense of contentment which does, in turn, have an effect on all those around you, for the better.

What's Next?

So, what is next for me in this life? After all the years of being raised in a strict Catholic upbringing, I am now a Humanistic Atheist and happily contented to declare it. I believe I still have a lot to contribute to society, to assist and support others to achieve a better life in the pursuit of their dreams, goals and aspirations. I will keep working while I believe I can continue to make a real difference for others and while I am still setting and achieving professional goals for improvements in the quality of life for women and children, and personal goals in my own life for the betterment of myself and my family.

I have a belief and commitment to lifelong learning and to supporting others, particularly women, in our community. My next goals are to participate on Boards of community organisations where I can contribute to the mission of that board and make a difference. I would also like to take up public speaking to inspire and motivate others, particularly women, to never give up on their life's dreams, goals and aspirations, until they achieve them. Everything is possible. If you can imagine it, it can happen.

Other than this I'm not exactly sure about what I will do next. I know I love learning and I love family and I love travelling with Gary and exploring the world, other cultures and other peoples. I love continuing to expand my worldview and will continue to learn until my last breath.

I do know I could never retire and do nothing. Retirement for me means cutting back on paid work, perhaps having an 'encore career' but not giving up work altogether. I like being connected to the world of work, connectedness to others and social welfare practice. I am very fortunate to have worked in so many fields of practice in my professional career, all of which have enabled me to meet new people, make new friends, taught me new life lessons and given me new depths of insight into the lives of other people.

The decision to write this book and bare my soul to all who read it was not one I took lightly. It is a daunting thing to do but I had been encouraged by several friends and family members, who know me well and know my story, to put it into words. Their motivations may have been because of pride in me or fascination with how my life has evolved but for me, the reason I chose to write this book became clearer to me only as I was writing it.

I came to realise in the beginning of my journey when I began to study at university, when my father was still alive, I was studying and striving to achieve in my life to spite him, to prove him wrong in his opinion of me. From all of my studies and professional experience I understand that all children, even as adults, want and need the approval of their parents. This is normal and is what I wanted at that time.

When he died after only one year of me studying, I had to ask myself, "Why am I studying now?" The answer came to me at that time. I was now going to do it for myself, not for anyone else, but to prove to myself that I could do it and succeed. I was determined to do so and this is what I did, in the end. I achieved it. I felt like an athlete who had scaled Mount Everest when I graduated with a PhD. It was a proud moment of achievement for me and my mother was there to see it and know that I could, and did, achieve that goal. I knew she was proud of me.

So, why write this book now? Now, I am doing it for others, to give forward, to let others know, in particular women, that no matter what others say about you or what they may think of you, you do not have to accept their appraisals as your truth. You can make choices to accept or reject those messages. You can set your own life's course, set your own goals and be the person you want to be. That is the message of my life to you and that is the purpose for writing this book.

What's Next?

I will leave you with one of my favourite quotes. It is from Mahatma Gandhi and it is simply to *"be the change you want to see"*.

"Gary and me now"

ABOUT THE AUTHOR

Dr Anne Butcher is a professional and qualified social worker who has worked in the not-for-profit sector and also within the Queensland Government. She has worked in both Central and North Queensland for most of her professional working life. She is also a wife, mother and grandmother who is passionate about her family. She is a strong advocate for human rights and social justice, particularly in relation to women and children, and she has held directorships on Regional, State and National Boards within Australia.

Her impressive professional career belies earlier life challenges which she had to overcome to go on and undertake a successful 23-year career in the Queensland Public Service. Anne's career has seen her span the fields of government investment and procurement with not-for-profit organisations, youth development, youth justice, child protection, disability services and seniors. Throughout these years her practice has developed from that of frontline social work practitioner to senior practitioner and then on to management and senior executive leadership roles.

For 16 years, while maintaining full-time work, Anne concurrently worked as an adjunct senior lecturer, sessional teacher and postgraduate research fellow within academia at both James Cook University and Central Queensland University.

Anne's career in the not-for-profit sector began in the small Central Queensland mining township of Dysart, where she worked as a Community Development Officer. Her career now, post public service, brings her again to work within charitable organisations. She currently holds the position of Executive Director for Mackay Women's Services. For the past few years, she has led a team of social welfare professionals who provide support and counselling services to women and children affected by domestic and family violence, and other services to women who benefit from a range of women's health and wellbeing programs.

Anne is a respected and professional motivational and inspirational public speaker who is often asked to speak to women's groups about her life and her career achievements to inspire and motivate others to achieve their life's goals and aspirations.

ACKNOWLEDGEMENTS

Just like anyone who is fortunate enough to achieve their life goals, I did not do it alone. Therefore, I would like to acknowledge those very important people in my life who have supported me, encouraged me, fed me and looked after me so I had the time and strength, emotionally and physically, to write this book.

Firstly, I would like to acknowledge my husband Gary who has always stood by me; despite the ups and downs which life threw at us, we are still as strong as ever. And to our children Ross, Brad and Heather, and our grandchildren whom I love with all my heart, I could not have written this book without the love and support you always give to me. Also, to my son Alan, who came into my life at a later time but who, along with his beautiful wife and two sons (my grandsons), have made my life so fulfilled and complete. Without you this book would not have been possible.

I would also like to thank Professor Ros Thorpe without whose guidance and mentorship, I have no doubt, I would not have accomplished as much as I have in my life. Professor Thorpe has also provided a testimonial for this book which I would also like to gratefully thank and acknowledge her for. Still supporting me as always.

Dr Amanda Nickson is a long-term friend and colleague who was the supervisor of my very first social welfare placement many years ago. She has shared in my life's journey and understands some of the challenges I had to face and overcome in my life. She also most graciously has presented a testimonial for this book which I thank her for most earnestly.

Another dear friend and colleague, Associate Professor Heather Lovatt, is a woman who I first met in the 1990s when we were both working for the State Government together. Heather and I have in many ways shared a parallel journey with careers, family similarities and academic trajectories. As Heather is very aware of many aspects of my life I asked her if she would write a testimonial for this book which she also very willingly obliged and I thank her most sincerely for her kind words.

I would like to acknowledge the photographer of the cover photo and friend, Catherine Zamparutti, for doing great work. I can't thank you enough. And, lastly but not least, I would like to sincerely thank the entire publishing team at 'Ultimate 48 Hour Author' without whose guidance, expertise and professional support the completion of this book would have been much more challenging than it was. You made it simple, you made it easy, you made it fun and I thank you all.

SPEAKERS BIO

Dr Anne Butcher is a wife, mother and grandmother. She is also a professional social worker with over 30 years of experience working in the social welfare fields of Community Development, Youth Development, Youth Justice, Child Protection, Disability Services, Women's Services—including domestic violence and sexual assault counselling services, and women's health and wellbeing programs. She has also been a social researcher and university lecturer, and is the author of academic journal articles, book chapters and books. She is regularly asked to speak at conferences or significant community events such as International Women's Day, or a range of other women's groups, service clubs, and many other community groups. Anne previously worked as an Executive Director, Manager and Leader, in both government and in not-for-profit organisations. She also has held positions as President, Director and Board member of National, State and Regional boards in Queensland and Australia.

She is passionate about seeing people, particularly girls and women, succeed in their lives and reach their fullest potential, whatever that may be for them.

Anne is a very warm, engaging, humorous and personable speaker who seeks to inspire others to achieve their life's dreams and goals through sharing her own life stories about work, study and family at her speaking events. Her speaking events are not to be missed and will leave her audience inspired to take action to achieve in their own life.

OFFERS AND CALL TO ACTION

Offer 1 To learn more about how to set your own life goals and take care of your own emotional health, I have prepared three short helpful videos for you to access, at no cost, on my website: drannebutcher.com

Offer 2 To stay up to date with any upcoming online and offline seminars, talks or events, visit drannebutcher.com/events

Offer 3 Engage Dr Anne Butcher as your event's next speaker!

Anne speaks on the following topics:

1. Communicating with confidence
2. Achieving your fullest potential
3. Overcoming barriers to succeed

To enquire about Anne's availability and rates, please email anne@drannebutcher.com

(Please note: Anne will speak to NFPs and some organisations for FREE so please mention your organisation when you enquire.)

NOTES

Notes

www.ingramcontent.com/pod-product-compliance
Lightning Source LLC
Chambersburg PA
CBHW070109120526
44588CB00032B/1393